Chios Island Travel and Tourism, Greece.
An Island Guide

Author
Michael Lopez

Information-Source Publishing Notice

INFORMATION-SOURCE. This book is strictly prohibited from any illegal or unauthorized digital or physical reproduction including photocopying, illegal distribution, Electronic/digital manipulation, without the prior written permission of the publisher. Information-Source publishing holds anyone failing to comply with the above mentioned responsible, and will be pursued under Copyright law.

Copyright © 2021 Information-Source Publishing
All Rights Reserved.

First Printed: 2021.

Publisher:
INFORMATION-SOURCE
16192 Coastal Highway
Lewes, DE 19958. USA.

Table of Content

CHIOS ISLAND ENVIRONMENTAL GUIDE 1
INTRODUCTION 1
THE HISTORY 5
TRAVEL AND TOURISM 12
Arrival in Chios 12
Chios-town 17
Mastika Villages 44
Kardamila and Northeast Chios 65
Volissos and West Chios 73
Chios Restaurants 83
Hotels in Chios 96
Top Things to see on Chios 104
Beaches in Chios 109
- Emporios Mavros Gialos beach 110
- Karfas beach 111
- Vrondados beach 112
- Agia Fotini beach 112
- Trahili beach 113
- Didima beach 114
- Lithi beach 115
- Megas Limnionas beach 116
- Agia Irini beach 116
- Apothyka beach 117
- Lampsa beach 118
- Lefkathia beach 119

Transportation to/from Chios 120
Things to See 122
- Medieval Castle 122
- Maritime Museum 124
- Chios Olympi Cave 127
- Oinousses Island 129
- Psara Island 131
- Monastery of Agia Markella 134
- Agios Markos Monastery 137

Villages 138

Chios Pyrgi 138
Chios Mesta 139
Chios Anavatos 140
Chios Volissos 142
Avgonyma 143
Agia Ermioni 144
Vrondados 145
Olympi 146
Emporios 149
Kampos 150
Kataraktis 151
Karyes 153
Kardamyla 154

Chios Island Environmental Guide

Introduction

Chios is an amazing island. Similar to Lesvos, it is one of those islands that you need a week or so to really explore, and then once you get to know it you will probably always want to go back. During my short visit to Chios I met people who spend every summer there, exploring the many walking trails and, remote beaches and villages. Compared to most of the Cyclades Islands, which are sort of one dimensional and interchangeable in that you see one, you have seen them all, Chios (and Lesvos) are islands where one village may be as different from the next as say an island in the Ionian is as different as one in the Aegean. I got off to a rough start and really was not happy with my first impression of Chios, at least until after a couple ouzos and I could see my experience with a sense of humor. More about that later. Someone who comes to Chios and does not get out of Chiostown may wonder why anyone would want to visit here, much less live here. But like any Greek town, or small city, no matter how much you may dislike it at first you always find some redeeming qualities. The traffic may be hell, the harbor may smell like sewage, and bad disco-rap-pop music may come pounding out of every bar, but you still can find a little place, a little corner of peace or beauty or maybe just good food and good people, that make all these other unpleasant things irrelevant.

But before you book your holiday in Chios town in the hopes of finding these little islands of pleasantness, the truth is that Chios town is where you have to go through to get to the <u>real</u> Chios, just like Pireaus is where you have to go through to get a ferry to the beautiful Aegean islands. The best part of Chios is the rest of the island. Amazing beaches, many with water the color of the Caribbean, scattered all along every coast , you could spend a month here and go to a different beach every day. I had five days to see them all and probably saw twenty or thirty. Some were full of people spending their weekend or holiday, while others were empty, one solitary car at the end of a dirt road. Usually mine. With beaches facing all four directions you can choose the type of sea you want. The wind is blowing from the north and you don't like waves? Go south. You like to body surf. Go north. You like snorkling? The island is made for you. You like to be surrounded by people while you are at the beach, there is that too.

The most unique thing about Chios is the area known as the Masticahoria, or the mastic villages which for hundreds of years have cultivated mastica, the sap of the mastic trees which was to the people of the Mediterranean and medieval Europe and the Middle East, what ginseng is to the Chinese and more. A wondrous substance that cures illnesses and has been used for a variety of purposes since ancient times. These fortified towns are like living in the middle ages, though of course you can stay in rooms with air-conditioning and the latest in technology and comfort. Mostly agricultural, these *masticahoria* are introducing ecotourism to the island. They are an important part of the future of Greek tourism. Their appeal is to people who don't want to just lay out on a beach soaking up sun and going to a bar at night to get drunk. The *masticahoria* are for people who see tourism as a process of self-education and see learning as fun. That does not mean they don't sunbathe or drink wine, or better yet, the local souma. It means they come for the whole package. Sun, sand, culture, history, great food, and most importantly the people.

The History

Chios is the fifth largest of the Greek islands situated in the North Aegean region. It is at the crossroads of West and East. From the magnificent mountains of the North to the protected valleys of the South, from the pristine shores of the West to the cosmopolitan resorts of the East, Chios arises from the merge of these antitheses imposing, stately and majestic. The

Chios strait, as it is referred to, separates the island from the Anatolian mainland and Turkey.

History of Chios

Archaeological traces indicate that Chios was inhabited as early as the Prehistoric Times. Its particular strategic position on maritime routes linking Eastern Mediterranean with the Black Sea and the island's proximity to the shores of Asia Minor led to its early settlement. <u>It is reportedly the birth place of Homer</u>, the legendary author of Iliad and Odyssey.

Prehistoric Period

Archaeological research provided evidence that Chios has been inhabited from the Stone Age to the present day. This is largely due to its location in the Easter Aegean just off the coast of Asia Minor from where it has been able to exploit the trade routes north to the Black Sea and south to the Mediterranean. The earliest settlements were established initially at Ayio Gala in the north and subsequently at Emporio in the South. Evidence has led scholars to content that the social distinction was feeble during that period as it appeared that all profited from agriculture and livestock.

Archaic and Classical Period

Chios was one of the original 12 member states of the Ionian League, a confederation of cities formed by the Ionian Greeks of Asia Minor at the end of the Meliac War. During the 7th and 6th century, the elements of political stability and economic growth led to the island's rise. During that time Chios exceled in arts and was also home of the renowned School of Sculpture. The government adopted a constitution that entailed democratic features, such as a people's magistrates (damarchoi) and a voting assembly, comparable to that of Solon. In 546 BC Chios was incorporated into the Persian Empire.

After an unsuccessful attempt to obliterate the Persian yoke by joining the Ionian Revolt in 499 BC, Chios was eventually freed in 479 BC at the Battle of Mycale, which essentially marked the end of the Persian Wars and subsequently joined the Delian League under the leadership of Athens. The Athenian-Chian relations were strong during that period as a result of Chios' benefits to Athens and its abiding loyalty. When Athens tightened its control of the city states Chios rebelled during the Social War (359-357 BC), as did Rhodes and later on others, demanding to be Athens's social and political equals and gained its independence until the rise of the rampant imperialism of Macedonia.

Hellenistic Period

Chios was conquered by Alexander in 332 BC and this marks the beginning of the Hellenistic Period of the island. During that time the island acquired much of its wealth through the export of wine – known to have been a pivotal economic activity for Chios. The quality of this wine was particularly fine and its reputation quickly spread throughout the Greek world. As attested by the Chian amphorae, the export of Chian wine has started during the early 6th century.

The Roman Period

The Treaty of Dardanos (85 BC) ended the First Mithridatic War between Pontus and the Roman Empire. It sealed the return to the status quo before wartime and consequently Greece belonged to Rome. There is some evidence that Chios was declared a free city by Sulla in 80 BC and Romans did not have authority over Chians in their city. Chios seems to have forged close relationships with Rome and this is corroborated by the fact that Gaius, heir of Emperor Augustus, and other Roman dignitaries have been associated with the island and that many Chians were awarded the Roman citizenship.

The Byzantine Period

After the fall of the Roman Empire, Chios was incorporated in the Byzantine Empire and developed to one of its leading economic centers. A hub of trade and commerce Chios exported its monopolistic products such as mastic, silk, wine and salt and imported grain and grew to a shipping power in the Mediterranean. The Empire reinforced the island's defensive capacity with fortresses and castles against the invading Arabs and Persians. The Byzantine Empire ceded trade privileges to the cities of Italy in exchange for services such as the Empire's naval reinforcement. During that period the competition between Chios and their Italian rivals who traded mastic extensively grew fierce.

The Genoese Period

The penetration of the Genoese to Chios is sealed with the Treaty of Nymphaeum (1261), a trade and defense pact signed between the Empire of Nicaea (the largest of the three Byzantine states) and the Republic of Genoa. The Empire cedes significant trade privileges to Genoa. In return the Republic would ally with the Empire in their effort to reconquer Constantinople. During this period the Genoese were more interested in trade and profit. They restructured the island both financially and military to obtain tight control of the trade posts and exploit the commercial revenues. The famous Maona was a company which monopolistically exploited the Gum Mastic and its obligation was to invest part of the proceeds to the island's defense system.

The Ottoman Period and Liberation

Chios became part of the Ottoman Empire in 1566. The Chians were granted a number of privileges, mainly in the form of tax exemptions, due to the cultivation of the mastic trees. The island developed marine sectors and trade routes to the Mediterranean and Black Sea. At the same time the School of Chios is founded. Chios is liberated from the Turkish yoke in 1912 and joins the rest of the Independent Greece.

Travel and Tourism

Arrival in Chios

After a wretched 3 hour journey from Lesvos on the hopefully scrapyard bound ferry Theophilos, the ramp slammed down and I drove my faithful

Suzuki Grand Vitara off the boat on to the dock of Chios town at 9:30 on a Friday night. I knew where the Chandris Hotel was, at the far end of the waterfront from where the ferry arrives, and all I had to do was follow the traffic off the ship and turn left. Wrong. The ship's traffic was directed up and into the city where we met up with more traffic of the local variety and we inched through the narrow streets.

Seeing an opportunity to go left and double back to the waterfront I took it only to discover that one lane of the two-way street that rings the harbor was blocked by a barricade and I was forced back to where I had begun my first journey on Chios, at the Theophilos. I tried again, this time with Andrea looking at a very un-detailed city may in the Rough Guide. The traffic was worse than New York. Worse than LA. Worse than I-40 in RTP. Even worse than Athens! "This road will lead us through the market" Andrea said as we took a right down a tiny street also clogged with traffic. Half an hour later we were out of the traffic but also out of the city on the road to Campo and its walled agricultural villages.

We turned around and looked for hopeful streets that might lead us back into Chios town and the area we wanted to be in. We finally arrived at the Chandris Hotel, an hour after we had gotten off the ferry which we could see a few hundred yards away across the harbor a 10 minute walk from the hotel. We parked in the lot that belonged to the bowling alley next door, completely empty since there were still spots on the sidewalks where you could park for free and the lot cost a euro to go in and a euro to leave. I left my car there all night to get my money's worth and we checked into the hotel.

Chios town from the Chandris Hotel Our room was on the 4th floor with a beautiful view of the harbor. There was a basket on the table filled with every kind of Chios product. Ouzo, figs, preserved fruits, and every type of mastika product from gum to toothpaste, body lotion and candies, weighing altogether about 50 pounds, a gift from Glikeria, the Chios representative of Hahathakis Tours. As we examined our treasures the phone rang. It was Glikeria inviting us to have dinner with her at Petrino, an ouzerie on the waterfront in an old stone mansion. We sat on the pavement as cars whizzed by, music and horns blaring.

The sidewalks were full of young people going to and from the loud bars that lined the street. It looked and felt like Saturday night in the East Village or Georgetown and half the voices were in English even though all the faces were Greek.

While Glikeria told us of the trials and tribulations of being a travel agent on an island that didn't even seem to want tourism we had the traditional mezedes of Chios, baked mastello cheese, local sausages and tomato-keftedes, drinking Apalarina one of the Chios ouzos, with the not entirely pleasant smell of the sewage filled harbor flavoring every bite and sip.

I typed a short text message to my daughter who had stayed in Lesvos: "This island sucks". I really meant it at the time. Luckily it got a lot better or there would not even be a Matt Barrett's Guide to Chios.

Chances are good that you won't arrive with a car and have to go through the ordeal I went through. If you are smart and have booked your trip to Chios through a Greek travel agency, they will send a representative to meet you at the boat and you can get a lift with someone who knows the traffic patterns of Chios-town. Or maybe you will just happily walk to your hotel, if you are staying in Chios-town. But you will need a car so if you want to avoid the terror of Chios traffic have it delivered to your hotel in the morning.

Chios-town

One day I will look at my trip to Chios as a shining example of my own special Greek island neurosis. For me to get off a ferry and not like an island at first is not abnormal. Its fairly typical actually. When I first went to Sifnos all the streets were torn up to make a trench for the sewage pipes with a pile of dirt that stretched the length of the harbor going past restaurants, cafes and shops which had boards as bridges to the tables where customers sat choking on the dust. My first impression was 'what kind of fked-up island is this? Yet it became one of my favorites. My first trip to Lesvos had me drinking ouzo morning til night just to survive and yet now it too is one of my favorite islands which I return to every year for anywhere from ten days to a month and usually have to force myself to leave. But after that first miserable night in Chios I was wondering how I was going to last four more and was there any way of going back to Athens without getting back on the ferry Theophilos.

Hotel Chandris, Chios, GreeceBreakfast helped. The Hotel Chandris is one of the last holdings of the once powerful Chandris family who used to own the largest cruise ship company in Greece. Now their fortunes have dwindled to a few luxury hotels, a 2% share of Celebrity cruises, and the Chios Chandris which though it is not luxury class, is a step above most hotels that you will find in the Eastern Aegean. A beautiful lobby and an even nicer restaurant and lounge area, the hotel also has a pretty nice swimming pool which hosts a Friday night buffet with live Greek music for its guests.

A large buffet breakfast had different styles of eggs, lots of breads and cakes, fruits, yogurt, bacon, sausage and pretty good coffee. (Andrea had a double espresso for 4 euros instead). Best of all right next door is a bowling alley. Yes. A bowling alley. I certainly can't complain about the view either since the photo was taken from our balcony. I would have been happy to sit on it all day and night, sipping ouzo and ordering room service while I wrote this entire site by copying bits and pieces out of the guidebooks like Hunter S Thompson covering the Superbowl by watching it on TV from his hotel room. But I would still have to go out eventually and take photos to go along with the guide so it was inevitable that I would have to leave the hotel sooner or later.

chiostown parkingIt turned out to be sooner. Fortified and ready for exploration we hit the streets of Chios town cutting up from the harbor to the central market and then down into the castle that contains the old city and its Turkish style houses, a hamam (Turkish baths though not working unfortunately), and enormous walls that rise from the moat, once filled with sea-water, now filled with cars. (It's a parking lot, though one of the more impressive parking lots you will ever see). The castle covers about 4000 square meters and was built by the Byzantines in the 10th century though the walls were later reinforced by the Genovese and the Turks.

Though many of the towers described in the writings of the middle ages no longer exist, the walls and gateways are impressive. The Turkish cemetery contains the graves of many notable Turks including Kapudan Pasa Kara Ali, the commander of the Turkish fleet that was destroyed by Kanaris in 1822 after the Turks had slaughtered the inhabitants of Chios. A nearby dungeon next to the Guistiani Museum is where the Turks held the civilian leaders of the island for 40 days before hanging them on April 23 1822. The neighborhood within the castle walls is where the Ottoman Turks and the Jews used to live.

cafeneon near Plastiras square in Chios townTraffic in the day was not as bad as traffic at night but in a way that was worse because everything moved faster and we were now on foot. Some town-planning might be in order. To make matters worse there is no road that bypasses Chios town. If you want to drive from southern Chios to northern Chios you have to drive back through the city, which adds to the traffic cars that don't even want to be there. Clearly the automobile is the downfall of Chios-town. There seems to be public transport and plenty of it. One of the best places to hang out in Chios is the bus station. Really.

There's a bar, and its air-conditioned and there are plenty of buses. But people in Chios-town, like in Athens, are in love with their cars despite the fact that they make the town a lot less livable for those who are on foot. But once you get used to the commotion Chios town is an OK place to be. There is a big central park, Voukianiou Square, with cafes and tables in the shade and a line of old style ouzerie-cafeneons where old men play backgammon, cards and even chess, while the proprietor serves ouzo, souma (tsipuro made from figs) and simple mezedes. On the north side of Voukianiou Square is a column which commemorates the leaders of Chios who in 1822 were hung by the Turks on that very spot.

Market in ChiosAt the east end of the square is an old Turkish Mosque with a tall minaret. The mosque now houses the Byzantine Museum. There is an old style central market with fish stalls, vegetables and even a loukamades shop as well as a couple working class restaurants. If you have never had loukamades you owe it to yourself to try them. They are deep fried dough blobs covered with honey and though they are probably not very good for your cholesterol count they are one of those things that when you find a place that makes them you should try them because they may not exist ten years from now.

When looking at Chios-town you have to keep in mind that most of the buildings were destroyed in the earthquake of 1881. Of the old buildings that did remain and the others that were built in the years following the earthquake, many of these were demolished to make way for modern apartment buildings. As in most places in Greece the local people did not realize that these old buildings of neo-classical or Smyrnian design were what made the town interesting and attractive, until it was too late and most of them were gone. But there are a few survivors and the town seems to have come to its senses and restoration projects are in evidence, especially in the old walled city within the kastro.

Chios WaterfrontThe waterfront cafes of Aegiou Street are where it all happens for the island's young people who start there with frappes in the morning and afternoon and mixed drinks in the evenings as the crowds spill out onto the sidewalks. Some are packed and some are empty. If you tried to figure out why one bar was successful while another was not you would have to assume that it is due to trends and has little to do with substance or the type of music they play. The most popular place was an Eastern looking bar with hookahs.

For my money the Beer Academy was the place to be, with several dozen international beers including some Belgian Trappist ales and Sam Adams. But in a country where beer drinkers are reluctant to venture beyond the triumvirate of Amstel-Hieneken-Mythos a beer hall may be doomed to failure were it not for the large number of Greek-American kids who come from all over the island to hang out in Chios town at night in the summer. Maybe this is why so many of the bars have a sort of seedy American style feel which I happen to find sort of comforting, like you could walk in, order a drink and have a long conversation with the guy next to you about the Mets or the Yankees or how Guiliani screwed the city and the firemen.

A large number of young soldiers hit the bars too since Chios is a border island. In the past Chios was a popular place to be stationed for obligatory military service. That's because all the men went to sea and left the women behind. "Ahhh Chios..." a former soldier reminisced. "I had ten girlfriends there at the same time. We all did." Its probably changed since then but the number of extraordinarily beautiful women walking the streets of Chios town at night was mind-boggling. If I was single and 10 years younger... (better make that 30 years younger), I imagine I would have a pretty nice time in Chios-town. Being there with my wife just made me feel old. Watching beautiful girls walking by dressed in their summer finest is just torturing myself. Still, is there anything more beautiful than a young woman dressed-to-kill out on the town on a Saturday night in Chios? Probably not.

Chios OuzoThere are several shops specializing in mastica products on the waterfront including the Mastic Spa with shops in all the major commercial centers of Greece as well as in New York, Montreal, Buffalo (?!!) and Toronto, where you can get everything from cosmetics to toothpaste, mastic gum and candy. There is also the Mastihashop which is owned by the Cooperative of Mastika Growers on Chios and has a wide variety of mastika products and information. Other shops sell traditional products from Chios including the many varieties of ouzo. There is also an excellent foreign press shop, perhaps the best in Greece with every magazine you have ever heard of in just about every language you have ever heard. It also sells guidebooks and maps of the island and has a very good English language book section. Of interest to any traveler who needs to keep up with current events and the baseball scores this is where you can get the International Herald Tribune, not to mention USA Today, the Athens News which comes out every Friday and arrives on the first plane of the day, and just about any other daily foreign newspaper. If you don't see it, ask and they probably have it. The waterfront also has many of the fastfood joints that you will find anywhere in Greece.

Tsibaeri ouzeriNear the derelict Rex Theater, a local icon which should be restored, are several fish tavernas and ouzeries where people eat while they wait for the ferry. We tried two of them but they all looked good. The menus at all of them were pretty similar. But in the past few years we have been going to the restaurant called Tsivaeri Ouzeri whenever we stop in Chios which is once a year. It is owned by a beautiful young couple and specialize in sun-dried spiced mackerel that is grilled, called gouna on some islands, but here it is called liasta. They make a deep-fried aferinia and onion cake which is also good.

Atherinia are the very smallest fish they catch. They also make it with shrimp (garithes). Tomato-keftedes (fried tomato balls), kolokethia-keftedes (zucchini-balls) and normal keftedes (meat balls) are popular. There are also a number for fried fish like gavros (anchovies), gopa (bream) and grilled sardines. The place I wanted to try but Andrea would not even consider it was the first restaurant which specialized in patsa and pizza, a very rare combination, patsa being tripe, the innards of a furry mammal and a health staple of the working class and pizza being... well, pizza. But thankfully we went to Tsivaeri and have been there so often they expect to see us every time the ferry from Lesvos stops in Chios. If you go say hello to Stavros and Vali.

Chios FerryBeyond the waterfront bars of Aigeou street and the restaurants on Neorion Street is the long breakwater pier and the building called the Bourtze, now a cafe-bar where the young people hang out. Its a great place to sit and watch the ships come in and out of the harbor, so close you could have a conversation with the passengers as they pass by. This is also where the ferry boats to Turkey leave from, in front of the customs house.

On hot summer nights this is where people without air-conditioning go to escape the heat of the city, some fishing from the end of the pier, others watching people fish and most of them in the Bourtze, drinking. Its a friendly place with young eager waiters and for those of us who love watching boats its a front row seat. Another nice spot to get away and enjoy a nice meal is Milarakia by the windmills in the photo at the top of the page. You have to walk left around the castle and then follow the road towards Vrontado to get there and it will take you at least a half an hour.

chios archaeology museumAs usual Andrea forced me to go to the Archaeological Museum ("Its your job Matt!!!") which nobody seemed to know where it was, even the people who lived right next door to it. It is hard to miss, a couple blocks up from the waterfront on Mixalon Street which actually starts off as Porfyra street near where the road turns towards the Chandris. The rear of the museum is actually on Museum Street which starts off as Souri Street. (Streets seem to do this a lot in Chios-town making getting around even more confusing.) By going the way of Museum Street which would seem to be the most practical way to find a museum, you have to go all the way around the grounds to find the entrance. Its a big modern building with a surprising number of ancient pieces and a very friendly staff that seem to outnumber visitors by five to one. What makes this museum special is that every item has a lengthy description in Greek and English, eliminating the need for a licensed guide, a good thing since there is only one on the island. Even the lengthy inscriptions on the marble tablets were completely translated, something you rarely see. Greek and Roman statues, a large collection of ancient coins and jewelry and household devices as well as pottery and even an entire ancient mausoleum make the Chios Archaeological museum a must for any visitor to the island and one of the best of all Greek island museums.

Statue in ChiosOther museums include the Maritime Museum, housed in a beautiful neo-classical mansion several blocks up from the port in a location that if I tried to guide you there would only confuse you. But if you walk up Neofytou Bamba Street and continue going straight until you reach Aplotarias Street, one of the main roads leading out of the city towards the south, make a left and start asking directions you may find it. I didn't. Better just stick with the

Archaeology Museum, the Byzantine Museum in the 19th century Ottoman mosque by the central square or the Guistiniani Museum by the central gate of the castle which features Byzantine frescoes, murals, icons and some Genovese art. If you walk up Korai Street from the center of the port you will come to a small square and on your left the Korais Library which houses the Argentis Ethnological and Folklore Museum.

In the summer there are a number of events from beach parties to big concerts in the Dimotiki Stadium across from the Archaeology Museum. While we were there Antonios Remos performed, his two giant 18 wheeler trucks making themselves a complete nuisance on the ferry home, clogging the entrance as they attempted again and again to back into the garage and causing the ferry workers to lose their tempers and take it out on the rest of us.

There are several Pireaus style skiliadiko nightclubs where you can see beautiful young popular music (laika) singers in sequins and cleavage being showered with champagne and rose petals til the sun comes up when everyone heads for the patsa joints to ward off today's hangover and be ready for the next evening. You will see posters splashed all over on poles, deserted buildings and even cars and trucks driving around covered in posters, announcing the event through a loudspeaker.

Within Striking Distance of Chios Town

Vrontados, ChiosChios Town is built on a long coastal plain backed by mountains. To the north is the village of Vrontados and to the south the beach village of Karfas. But the term village is not really accurate because pretty much all the land between these 'villages' has been built up turning them into beach suburbs of Chios town. Karfas is known as the resort area of the island. So we skipped it. Vrontados has some nice old mansions and narrow winding streets as well as a couple beaches. But beaches in cities are really for the inhabitants and are popular out of convenience, not because they are particularly nice beaches. People who live nearby can walk to them. But someone visiting the island of Chios would not put the beaches of Vrontados on their 'things to do' list.

Karfas, ChiosKarfas is another story they say. Its not my kind of place but if you like small to medium sized family run hotels, decent tavernas, a long sandy beach and lots of people on weekends and in August then you can check it out and let me know what I missed since I was only here long enough to take this photo. If you are used to the popular beach towns in Crete or the Cyclades then Karfas will seem pretty laid back in comparison. But by Chios standards it is what you would call a 'tourist beach' though then tourists will probably be mostly Greek or Greek-American, Australian or whatever.

As for swimming in Chios Town.... well people do it. (mostly people in their nineties who probably always swam there and always will) That does not mean that I would or you should. Swimming in or near any big city won't kill you. It may be healthier than not swimming at all. But the general rule for me is that when you are in a city the sea is for looking at while having lunch or an ouzo, not for swimming. When you want to swim you drive as far from the city as you can. If you don't drive? Don't stay in the city. In fact even if you do drive don't stay in the city. There are more interesting places to stay on Chios and you can see what you need to in town in a couple hours.

The area called Kampos is a collection of agricultural villages that like Vrontados to the north have become almost a suburb of Chios town. A lush area of citrus trees and walled mansions, some as old as the 14th century, Kampos is the most fertile area of the island and is also known as Lalades for its many tulips. It is said that the Dutch first brought back tulips from here to Holland where they began cultivating them. Now the Municipality of the Kampochora with the cooperation of the Univerisity of the Aegean Department of the Environment is taking steps to reclaim the tulip, perhaps designating Chios as 'Land of the Tulips' and incurring the wrath of Holland who will join the Italians of Genoa who are angry at Chios' claim to be the birthplace of Christopher Colombus and invade the island. Hopefully not though it should inspire some of the more curious Dutch tulip lovers to come for a visit.

Argentikon Hotel, ChiosAt one time there were over 200 estates here but many of fallen into decay. Many of the remaining mansions have been restored to their former splendor and some like Argentikon Palatial Estates have been turned into traditional inns. This estate is a luxury hotel with five individual villas, in the kind of surroundings that kings and queens are used to with exotic gardens a large pool and a restaurant, all in buildings that date back to the 1500s. Most walls and buildings of Kampos are built from the local red stone from Thymiana.

The high walls hide lush gardens and pebbled mosaic patios, grape arbors and giant pine and cyprus trees. The town of Ag Giorgos Sycoussis named after the monastery of Saint George and the Sycous civilization which inhabited the area, is one of the most affluent villages in Kampos and offers a nice view of the kampos (plain) below. It also has a local souma festival organized by the municipality. Vassileoniko has a number of churches, citrus orchards and a festival to Saint Panteleimon on July 27th. This saints day is also celebrated in the village of Dafnonas which is also known for its ouzo distillery. Vavili has a Byzantine museum and some Genovese mansions that are still standing and also the Catholic Church of Saint John. In the Church of the Ypapanti Virgin you will find icons painted by Hawaiian artist Juliette May Fraser.

In Kallimasia is the 19th Century Monastery of the Pagagia Plakidiotissa. The Folklore Museum of Kallimassia has preserved village customs by constructing an ouzo still, olive oil press, blacksmith, tailor shop, shoemaker's shop and Karagiozis. Their objective is to eventually create an entire early 20th century traditional village. The Popular Art Cooperative of Kallimasia has a shop which sells traditional embroideries, traditional Chios costumes, dolls, sheets and bed covers.

There is frequent bus service to Karfas, the island's beach resort as well as the beaches of Agia Ermioni, Megas Limionas and Agia Fotia. Near the village of Neochori is the Agios Minas Monastery where in 1822 the Ottoman Turks slaughtered several thousand Chiotes. It also has a terrific view. In Thymiana the carnival known as Mostra takes place during the last days of Apokreas with men dressed in island costume dancing the talimi, reenacting the battles between the people of Chios and the pirates during the middle ages.

Cars and motorbikes can be rented on the waterfront in Chios at a number of different places. Keep in mind that Chios is a big island and more suited to cars than motorbikes. There are also the famous red Chios taxis which can get you to many of these places at a reasonable (even negotiable) rate.

Finally...

North of ChiosFor those of you who are passing through Chios on your way back to Pireaus from Lesvos you have an hour to get off the boat and explore. (Check this with the boat because it may vary with the ferry and the season but every time I have stopped in Chios we had an hour.) In early August there is a festival in the Public Gardens above Voukaniou Square just a couple blocks up from the waterfront on Kanari street. It features local dances, free food and free ouzo, plus lots of art and local crafts and many of the people involved are Greek-Americans who are happy to tell you what they love about their island.

Make your way up Kanari Street which should be the street that ends near the front of your ferry (You will know what I mean when you get there.) Walk up Kanari until you reach the main square and the Public Gardens are beyond. If its not August and there is no festival walk along the waterfront and buy some mastica products, or go have an ouzo and mezedes at Tsivaeri Ouzeri by the Rex Theater or across from Pastiras Square. It was this festival that made me want to return to the island and spend more time here. Don't let what I have written about Chios-town deter you from visiting Chios. It just takes getting used to or being prepared (or something). Anyway you can't get to the rest of Chios without going through it unless you know how to fly.

Mastika Villages

The best part of Chios and what makes the island unique is what are known as the mastikahoria, the famous mastic villages of Chios. These are a series of fortified villages built in the 14th century during Genovese rule (1346-1566). These villages had an economy based on the cultivation of mastic, a gum like sap from the mastic trees that are unique to the island and were so prized that the Genovese built fortresses to protect them, and when the Turks massacred the inhabitants of Chios, the mastic villages were spared.

Of these villages the most impressive are Pirgi with its intricately painted houses, Olympi and Mesta which are both medieval fortress towns pretty much intact. These villages were built out of sight from the sea and surrounded by high walls with a central tower that was the last resort in case the walls were breached by the Arabic pirates who raided the coasts of the Mediterranean. The tower had no door at street level but was entered by ladders which were used as bridges from the rooftops and then pulled up. The tower had three floors and in the case of Mesta an underground tunnel that led to the well so that even in a siege water would be available.

Pirgi, ChiosThe streets were also designed for defensive purposes, narrow and dark with blind alleys that would not only confuse the invaders but enable the villagers to attack them from above using the walkways and arches that connected the buildings. The houses themselves were small individual fortresses and were an essential part of the whole castle and defensive system. The ground floor has one entrance and no windows. The animals lived downstairs. The main characteristic of the house is the pounti, a sort of patio on the first floor reached by a staircase which led to the sleeping areas, usually two bedrooms. The pounti had a ladder that went to the roof. In the case of an invasion the ladder could be pulled up and the villagers could walk to the central tower for protection. The roofs of the village were also used for drying almonds or for sleeping out on hot summer nights. These fortress towns were based on the designs of the ancient Greek towns of Ionia.

Pirgi is the largest of these mastic villages. Its outer wall is mostly gone enabling the village to creep out beyond its former boundaries. Like the other fortified villages there was a central tower. In Pirgi the tower still exists and sections of it have been turned into residences. Above the main square is the church of Kimissis Tis Theotokou (Our Lady's Dormition), a three-aisle basilica built in 1694. Just off the main square down a small covered alleyway is the 13th Century church of Agios Apostoli with its frescoes, painted by Domestihos Kinigos of Crete. This church is one of the oldest and most visited on the island. It is a copy of Nea Moni, the famous monastery in Chios. There are two other churches in the village worth visiting, Taxiarchis, which was built in 1680 and Ipapanti which is even older. The main square has a beautiful old cafeneon run by an old Greek-American from Astoria who serves an excellent mezedes with his ouzo.

pirgi, chios, greeceThe most interesting feature of Pirgi are the decorative designs scratched into the exterior walls of the houses, known as ksista. Mostly geometric forms, ksista has gone through several periods and may have originated in Genoa or in Constantinople. The process, which is still practiced today, even on the modern buildings of the village, begins with the spreading of a mixture of sand, asbestos and cement on the walls of the house. This is then covered with white asvestis (No, not the poisonous asbestos, in Greece asvestis means lime. If you want to say asbestos it is amiantos). When it dries the patterns are drawn onto the outer layer and then scratched with a fork to reveal the darker layers beneath. The whole village is covered in these designs, including some of the churches and the local bank. Another feature of the village are the tomatoes which hang drying beneath many of the balconies of Pirgi, adding a splash of color to the back and white designs on the houses.

Christopher Columbus house in Pirgi, Chios, GreecePirgi is the ancestral home of Christopher Columbus, according to the locals, and what is said to be his house , just off the main square, had a plaque placed there by the European Union, that since my visit has been removed for whatever reason, maybe due to complaints by Italians. It is accepted that he lived here for a time. But was Columbus from Chios as many people from Chios and even a few scholars believe? This seems a likely possibility.

If you were Queen Isabella who would you be more willing to trust to find a route to the east and give three ships and the equivalent of a few million dollars to? The peasant son of a wool-worker from Genoa, or a Byzantine seaman (or prince as some people believe) from the island of Chios? There are still many people in Pirgi whose last name is indeed Columbus or Couloumbos. It is known that many of his crew were Greeks, many of his friends as well and that the notes he wrote in the margins of his books were also in Greek. Furthermore he wrote about the island of

Chios and the healing properties of mastic. The people of Genoa may not like the idea that Columbus came from Chios since they have made a fortune off him in tourism but if you look at the evidence you have to admit that Chios should be at least considered as the new Mecca for Columbofiles, if there is such a thing anymore.

Columbus has dropped in popularity since the days when I was in elementary school and Columbus Day was a holiday. In fact many people hate him now because of the atrocities he committed against the native Americans. But that is all besides the point when the question is was he from Chios or Genoa, since being from one place or the other would not change anything. Personally I don't care but there are people who do and have written books about it and even have a society dedicated to this theory which you can read about here: Click for more about Columbus and Chios

Olymbi, chios, greeceJust down the road from Pirgi is Olympi one of the most impressive of the mastikahoria. The outer wall of this village is still intact though windows and doors have been cut into them. There is a beautiful little square and a couple of cafeneon-restaurants and the church of Agia Paraskevis. The central tower is still standing though in ruins. A few kilometers down the road is the Cave of Olympi, with the largest number of stalagmites and stalactites per square meter of any cave in the Balkans. The cave was discovered in the hole where the villagers used to throw their dead animals and is still being explored. You can do a twenty minute tour which goes every hour or so from 11:00 to 18:00 every day except Monday. You may notice some interesting billboards on the road between

Olympi and the caves and you may be curious as to what they are all about. What they basically say is that if you see something metallic don't pick it up. The area was used in the past for military target practice and there may be unexploded shells around. So rather than wander in the hills and risk getting blown up take the road to the small beach at Fani and on the way stop at the ruins of the Sanctuary of Apollo Phaneos and the small church built on its foundation.

Mesta

mesta, chios, greeceMy favorite town in Chios is Mesta, a completely intact fortress town of 300 people, the best preserved of the mastic villages, a living history and cultural museum where life goes on the way it has for hundreds of years. In the Turkish genocide of 1922 many of the inhabitants were captured to be used as slaves.

Because mastic was so important a product, those who knew how to grow and process it were freed and sent back to the village. In 1858 the defensive tower which was no longer considered necessary was demolished to build the Church of the Taxiarchis, still the largest church in Chios.

It overlooks the main square which has two cafes and the very good taverna O Meseonas, owned by the lovely Despina Bournia, who along with Anna Floradi is very active in promoting the village. The restaurant has a varied menu that features many local Chios dishes such as their tomato keftedes, local cheese and my favorite discovery of the trip, souma, a drink made from figs that is similar in taste and potency to raki or tsipuro. (Or moonshine if you are from the southern United States).

Besides Despina's taverna in the main square there several cafes and there are two or three psistaria-pizza places outside the village walls. The older church of the Taxiarchis from the 4th ort 5th century contains a number of frescoes and wood carvings of scenes from the Old Testament and the life of Jesus. This church was actually a monastery and the village grew up outside its walls, eventually enclosing itself in the outer walls.

Vasilis Bellas, Chios MasticultureTwo people leading the way in Chios eco-tourism are Vassilis Ballas and Roula Boura who left their desk jobs in Athens to come to Chios to create their vision which they called Chios Masticulture, teaching Greeks and tourists about the cultivation and production of mastic as well as other traditional activities. Vassilis took us out to the mastic orchards outside the village and showed us the whole process of extracting and collecting the mastic. Additional activities they provide in their tours include creating a garden of organically grown local vegetables, visiting local wineries and other agricultural processing plants and bee hives, joining local fishermen in fishing expeditions, and hiking around the countryside where, depending on the season, they pick mushrooms and local herbs.

They also help with room bookings, ferry tickets, and car rentals, organize conferences, business meetings, and other events for professional organizations and businesses, in indoor and/or outdoor village locations appropriate for group events. Most importantly they educate visitors on the cultivation and production of mastika. Masticulture puts together ecotourism packages that combine hospitality and outdoor activities related to all the things that compose the culture of Chios: its customs and traditions, popular arts and crafts, agricultural labour and produce, architecture, and much more.

mesta, chios, greeceMesta is one of those perfect villages for families. There are several gates into the town, none wide enough for a car so kids are safe to play in the streets. We stayed in the Anna Floradi Apartments, which are traditional rooms in one of the medieval dwellings. We also were given a tour of the Medieval Castle Suites, a collection of houses scattered around the village that have been renovated into luxury apartments with air-conditioning, full kitchens, stereos, Internet and satellite television.

There are numerous trails to hike including many that lead to the beaches and the path between Mesta and Olympoi that goes past the church of Ag Antonios as well as the old aqueduct and stone wells. With the cultural and educational activities provided by Masticulture and the Cultural Association of Mesta there is no reason why you or your family should worry about there not being enough to do here. But just in case let me add that Mesta is also known for the large number of religious and cultural celebrations throughout the year.

Apokreas (carnival) is a fun time to be in Mesta with parties in the village and the main square. On Clean Monday they have a popular court of justice in the square. Based on a tradition that dates back to the occupation when the Turkish Pasha enforced his own laws with harsh penalties, the trials satirize this period with crazy accusations of 'crimes' that villagers have supposedly committed which they then have to stand trial for while standing before an older member of the village dressed as the Pasha who metes out punishments based on the accused's financial status. People come from all over Chios for these trials.

"At the Carnival, in Mesta and some other of the island's villages revives the custom of "Agas". Its roots go back to the period where the Aga (the ottoman tax collector) would visit the village to collect the taxes in mastic. Nowadays the event is a humorous and recreational festival that coincides with the closing of the carnival. The celebration starts with a parade from the old school outside of the village to the central square. At the Village's Gate a small battle is being performed as the Agas and his crew riding donkeys are trying to invade the village.

They arrive in the central square accompanied by locals dressed in traditional costumes playing music instruments and singing old songs and "amanedes". During the trial Agas who is a very strict judge judges and condemns the most of the people that are present. More over, they are obligated to buy off their sentence, otherwise the Agas orders his officers to beat them up. The sessions are interrupted by music and dances by the folk dance group of the village or the locals and the visitors. The event is hosted by the cultural association of the village. It is one of the oldest and most interesting custom of Chios Island and is revived in Mesta and other villages. The first time we had this event was around 1830 to 1840." Vassilis Ballas

Souma, ChiosDuring Easter there is a big fire in the square and an effigy of Judas is burned. (They used to hang him from a tree outside the village and shoot at him). There are also a number of feasts on the saints days of the village churches including August 1st when everyone goes to the small island of St Stefanos and celebrates til dawn. On August 8th the celebration of St Aimilianos takes place on the beach of Merikounda and again lasts through the night. On the 11th of August the town of Mesta hosts the Festival of Souma, the above-mentioned alcoholic drink made from figs. A giant distiller is set up in the square and people drink the souma and dance all night long. On August 17th is the Festival of the Fishermen with a fishing contest in the morning and fish soup at night. On November 8th people come from all over Chios for the saint day of the Great Taxiarchis and on the 11th the whole island is celebrating its liberation in 1912 when Chios officially became part of Greece.

chios beachThere are a half dozen or so beaches within twenty minutes drive from Mesta which

South west side of island

range from beautiful to spectacular. Because some of the beaches are protected from the north winds and others from the south, you can always find a beach to enjoy regardless of the weather conditions. At Agia Dynami you will find some of the most beautiful turquoise water you will see anywhere in Greece and Agia Theodocia monastery which has a covered picnic area where people escape the sun and eat their lunch. Trahilia is a narrow peninsula with a beach on either side that leads to a rocky island that is terrific for snorkeling. There are a handful of fishing boats that are based here. You can reach these beaches by footpath or on the paved (and unpaved) roads that wind through the olive and mastika groves. Other beaches worth spending the day include Avlonia, Apothika, Merikounta, and Potami.

mesta, chios, watchtowerThe coast is dotted with a series of Genovese watchtowers known as vigles which warned the people of Chios of any impending attacks by pirates. These towers were around 15 meters high with the entrance on the second floor. The Vigla at the port of Mesta is one of the most intact and can be reached on foot from Mesta through the pine forest. These vigles were within sight of each other so by going to one you can look up and down the coast and see them in series. Another mostly intact tower is the one at Didima just 2 kilometers north of Limenas, the port of Mesta. The port itself is in transition, having received money from the EU to make it able to handle larger boats since it is closer to the mainland and the Cyclades islands than the port of Chios town which faces Turkey. Limenas has a small tree shaded beach and some rooms to rent as well as the popular fish taverna O Sergis.

emporio, chios, greeceIf you have a week to spend in Chios my advice would be to base yourself in Mesta for at least 3 of those days and use the town to explore southern Chios. Otherwise go to Emborio near the southeast tip of the island. The town is believed to be the ancient Leukonion mentioned by Thucidides and excavations have unearthed a temple to Athena and other buildings including a sanctuary to the Goddess near the harbor below. Over fifty houses have been excavated and as work continues they expect to uncover more.

The extinct volcano of Psaronas rises next to the modern village and is the cause of the black pebble beaches of Mavros Gialos and Foki which are similar to the famous black sand beaches of

Santorini. They are among the most spectacular beaches in all the Greek islands and on summer weekends draw a crowd so either get out of town by then or use Sunday to explore the rest of the island and return to your hotel on Sunday evening when all the kids have gone. The Hotel Emporio Bay is excellent and is the kind of friendly family run establishment that keeps people returning year after year. The hotel has a pool, not that you need it with such great beaches nearby. There are several good fish tavernas right in the town overlooking the sea including Posidonas and Emporios which both feature fresh local fish and ouzo and mezedes as well as other classic Greek dishes. Nearby villages worth visiting are Armolia, famous for its pottery and the 15th century Castle of Apolyhnon. The 18th century Zoodochos Pygi Monastery was an important spiritual-intellectual center but was destroyed ion the massacres of 1822. It was restored in 1828 and now is the home to exactly one monk. The town of Kalamoti is one of the largest of the mastikahoria and the nearby beach of Komi one of the best in Chios. map p 146

Kardamila and Northeast Chios

Our last day we planned to leave from Emporio and drive to the north of Chios as far as Kardamila and then return to catch out ferry at 10pm. Unfortunately there is no ring road around Chios town so you have to go back into the traffic hell and then out again, which we did, stopping only long enough to buy some Hyundai AA batteries for my camera which worked exactly ten seconds. We drove along the coastal road by abandoned factories and Lo Beach, which is the public beach of Vrontados, past the signs that advertised Daskalopetra or Homer's rock where he supposedly taught his students.

The Monastery of Mersinidi located on a rock high above the sea is known for the ships that passed below, sounding their horns to greet the Panagia (Virgin Mary). We passed the tiny Glaroi Beach in a small cove that looks like it is in danger of being swallowed up by the nearby quarry. To our right was the island of Inousses (actually several islands clustered together between Chios and Turkey) which is known for the large number of sea captains who have houses there. Our first stop was a small bay between Lagada and Vrontados that was full of derelict boats, some half sunken, some being worked on, the kind of places I love though about as friendly as a junkyard full of Dobermans.

Lagada, ChiosWe took a few photos and continued on to the village of Lagada, a small port at the end of a fertile gorge that has a small river lines with fishing boats. There is a footbridge over the river that goes to a tree shaded beach. There are a number of fish tavernas in the town which stretches along the sea for several hundred meters. Its an idyllic spot for lunch or dinner and not a long drive from Chios town. But we cut inland to a small town in the center of the island called Pityos where there was reputed to be a fantastic taverna in a platanos tree covered square that was famous for its traditional food, in particular the hand made pasta. Pityos is a small agricultural town with a round castle on a hill in the middle of it.

Not much reason to go there except for the Markellos Taverna, which was as good as advertised and full of Greek tourists and Chiotis who had also driven here for lunch. Not that they had to drive. The bus stopped right in front of the taverna. I had the goat in tomato sauce, while Andrea had the famous macaroni with fresh tomato sauce and local cheese. We also had stuffed zucchini flowers, the island's famous tomato-keftedes (like meatballs but flat and made with tomatoes and flower instead of meat), and my staple, a Greek salad and sadziki. While we ate the women who ran the restaurant were rolling and stuffing dolmades and getting ready to make the handmade pasta.

kardamila, chios, greeceOur nest stop was the port of Kardamilla, famous for the number of men who took to the ships. In the port there is a statue of a Greek sailor going to sea and just down the road on a small islet a statue representing the women of Kardamilla, gazing out to sea. During the middle ages Kardamilla was the largest village on the island. It played an important role in the Revolution of 1821 and supposedly was never captured by the Turks. It is now famous for the many ship-owners who come from here. Kardamilla is not a town that you would call tourist friendly though I would not say it is unfriendly. It is indifferent.

But any tourist venturing this far will find some nice cafes, fish tavernas, some beautiful old houses in the lower and upper village, and lots of English spoken. The place is crawling with Greek-Americans, many who are here for the summer and some who have retired in their ancestral village. The port was full of yachts, along with a few fishing boats. There was one junta-style hotel on the beach that looked like the owners had given up on the outside, but I am guessing that any guests here are overflow from the family house.

kardamila, chios, greeceThe upper village was the kind of place I would want to retire to, similar to the traditional villages of Lesvos. The village had a stream that ran beneath the giant platanos tree that covered main square, dry in the summer but I imagine it can run pretty fiercely in the winter. There were two traditional cafeneons/tavernas, one run by an old man who was doing his best to sweep way the leaves that had fallen that day from the trees. The other seemed to be run by kids who were playing a video game or something while the TV blared in the background. But outside both cafes, old men sat drinking coffee and talking, sometimes dropping English words and phrases into their conversation. While Andrea organized the car so she would not have to do it in some hot parking lot in Athens, I drank a Kampos Cherry Soda, made of course in Kampos, Chios.

MMichalis Markos Xylas, kardamila, Chios, GreeceI actually do have a connection to the town of Kardamilla. In 1978 I sailed from New Haven, Connecticut to Genoa, Italy on the ship the Giorgos Xylas, carrying scrap metal. It was one of those character-defining journeys where you discover whether you are cut out for a life at sea. I wasn't. It was so boring that if I was playing solitaire I would attract a crowd of ten or more crewmen, all shouting advice, turning a simple and unimportant game to pass the time into a stressful situation similar to batting with the bases loaded in the last of the 9th with two outs in Little League.

The ship was owned by Michalis Markos Xylas who was a patron of the village and whose statue sits outside the church in the upper village. If you lack purpose in your visit to this part of Chios a visit to the statue should fill the void and give meaning to your trip or an excuse to visit the upper village. Kardamilla really felt like I was somewhere familiar. In fact we got to know the village even better after we left. Andrea lost all her keys while cleaning out the car in the square and for the next few weeks several calls went back and forth to the cafeneons in a fruitless search for them. Also of interest in Kardamilla is The Snoopy Center where aspiring young dog actors train to play Snoopy in the next Peanuts movie.

Nagos, ChiosBeyond Kardomilla are a series of rocky beaches which when the north wind is blowing have some pretty big waves and some sheltered wooded coves which don't. There is also a spring at the side of the road near Nagos I believe. Andrea wanted to stop and wash the car there but I didn't. First of all it was a narrow road and I could have gotten killed doing it. Secondly, I like the way the Vitara looks covered in dust and mud. "That's how a 4-Wheel-Drive is supposed to look." I told Andrea. "Like you have been out in the wilderness exploring, not like you have just taken a trip to the mall".

You can continue to follow the road around the northeast part of Chios which connects at Katavasi with the road from western Chios back to Vrontados and Chios-town. We didn't. We went back by way of Langada and Pontoukos past a number of fish farms, ending up back in Chios-town with a few hours to spare before catching our ferry to Pireaus. We could have stopped at Homer's Rock. That would have been the responsible thing to do as a travel writer. But we didn't. Sorry.

Volissos and West Chios

From the traffic-clogged streets of Chios Town you follow the overhead signs towards Avgonyma. Escape is fairly easy once you get past the market area near the port and before you know it you are in the country climbing a pretty steep mountain. First stop is Nea Moni or New Monastery, about 15 kilometers from Chios town. Started by three hermits the monastery is the home of the miracle-working icon of the Theotokos which was found hanging from a tree. The monastery was begun by Constantine the Combatant who was the emperor of Byzantium and completed by the empress Theodora.

Decorated with mosaics from the best artists of the 11th Century, many of which survive, the monastery was attacked by the Turks in 1822, its inhabitants slaughtered, and again in 1828. This is one of the most important and interesting religious and national historical sites in Greece and should not be missed for it contains some of the finest examples of religious art in the churches and the museum on the premises. The bones of those killed in the massacre can be seen in the Chapel of the Holy Cross, also within the monastery. One small piece of information. It is advertised as open all day. Its not. Its closed from 1 to 4. We only got to see it from the outside. Go in the morning.

<u>Anavatos, Chios, Greece</u>Past the 11th century village of Avgonima and the island's only Paint Gun Battlefield (listed under eco-tourism for some odd reason in one of the island guides) you come to the (nearly) deserted village of Anavatos in one of the most dramatic settings of any village in Greece. Perched precariously on a large granite rock on the edge of a cliff, the town was attacked by the Turks in 1822. The inhabitants threw themselves Masada style from

the cliff rather than be taken prisoner or butchered. In 1881 the earthquakes that destroyed much of Chios damaged the buildings that had survived. A restoration project has been underway for a number of years and you can walk through the (almost) deserted town. With few survivors there was nobody to repopulate the village and the town has become a national monument. But there are people living here as you will notice as you walk through the streets and see some buildings with doors, and even gardens.

Maria Sarri painting, chios, greeceOne of the inhabitants is the artist Maria Sarri whose beautiful house overlooks the small church at the entrance of the village and has one of the most tastefully decorated gardens you will ever see. One of Greece's most beloved artists she has exhibited all over the world and received many awards. Works of her embellish airports and tourist agencies of Europe and decorate the Ecumenical Patriarchate, the Archdiocese of Athens, and the offices of both the President of the Republic and the Prime Minister as well as other public and private places. There is a small cafe-restaurant in Anavatos as well as an information booth. But if you are like me you will head for the sea and a swim before stopping for lunch.

Chios BeachBetween Lithi and Volissos there are a number of beaches. Some like Trachili and Xeropotamos with pebbles and white sand in small coves so blue you can't wait to dive in, others less inviting in terms of color though more interesting if you like snorkeling like Papalia, Gerita and Prastia near the town of Sidirounta. At Papalia there is a small island you can walk to and the rocks make it a good spot for snorkeling and according to the people at the dive shop in Chios town a terrific place for spear-fishing.

In Metochi Bay there is a stone beach and a small fish taverna right on the road overlooking the sea that is a popular place to stop that served simple island food and fresh fish. If you want to hold on a little longer continue past the long beach of Managros and follow the signs to Limnos (not to be confused with Limnaria which is right next door) just below the town of Volissos and have lunch at the Limnos Restaurant, right on the beach. Its a clean and well-run place with good food and friendly service.

Volissos, Chios, GreeceVolissos is the ancient city of Voliskos, built on the side of a hill and crowned by a Byzantine castle built by General Velissarius, the leading Byzantine general during the reign of Emperor Justinian I. The city was a center of commerce during the middle ages and after the fall of Constantinople many members of the Byzantine aristocracy moved here. It is also said to be the birthplace of Homer. The town is a labyrinth of narrow streets and alleys paved with the pebbles from nearby beaches.

In the last few years foreigners have taken an interest and begun buying up the old houses of the village. Its not a bad place to have a house since the nearby beaches are among the best in Chios with the closet one, Managros in Volissos Bay, being one of the longest on Chios. Volissos has hotels, restaurants, rooms to rent, car rentals and many other tourist facilities though it is far from being a tourist town, so far. If you are looking for somewhere to stay Volissos Holiday Homes offer self-catering accommodations with sea-view, free Wi-Fi and it is within walking distance of Lefkadia beach.

Chios UnexploredVolissos is also the home of Isidoros Tsouros, Ecotourism Operator and founder of Chios Unexplored. Isidoros (known as Sideris by the locals) was born in Athens. In 1992, he made the decision to move to Chios and fulfil his dream. For the next 20 years, Sideris built up a remarkable career as a Lawyer and he was elected President of the local Bar Association twice. In 2005, Sideris purchased a very small but beautiful stone farmhouse called Mourkia, located on the top of a hill outside Volissos village in Chios, Greece. It has been renovated with care for simplicity and respect to its traditional plan. In 2012, a few years after the crisis hit Greece, Sideris migrated to London.

However, he never really managed to "fit in" and be socially integrated into the new environment. He frequently felt homesick and that feeling was growing inside of him as time went by. Finally, in

2015 he returned to Chios, determined to get involved with everything that made him happy and whole as a person: The wider Amani area with its traditional architecture and the impressive stone structures, the rare flora and fauna of the island, the old pathways, paleontological findings, deserted beaches and the traditional cooking using local products.

His company Chios Unexplored makes the most of the island's potential in collaboration with excellent local young experts, in a way that the visitors can experience activities that will leave a positive environmental and social footprint. Activities that are authentic and original and give the opportunity for visitors to experience aspects of the island that cannot be found in tourist guides but, are well known by the locals.

Further north on another long beautiful beach is the Monastery of Agia Markella with its miracle working icon. The panagiri for the monastery is held on July 22nd and is the biggest on the island. People come from all over Greece to celebrate. Further north, about as far north as you can get are the healing waters of the Hot Springs of Agiamata which are said to be very helpful for people suffering from rheumatism. In the town of Agio Galas is a small church called Panagia Agiogalousena built at the entrance of an impressive cave.

Vrontados, Chios, GreeceYou can go back to Chios-town by taking the road from Katavassi which passes through some of the most barren landscape that you will find anywhere. Dotting the miles and miles of bare mountains are these squares of pine forests, each with a name of the organization or people who have sponsored the planting and watering of the trees. Some are twenty years old and others were planted in the last couple of years. The road reaches the end of the mountain known as Marathovouno and begins a series of hair-raising turns that eventually bring you back to the town of Vrontados, just north of Chios town. But before you get to the bottom, at the first opportunity stop and enjoy the view of the east coast from Vrontados to Chios-town.

Chios Restaurants

There are two kinds of Greek restaurants. Well there are more but for the sake of this page lets say there are just two. Those that are for Greeks and those that are for non-Greek tourists. Chios, being a Greek island, the type that does not get many foreign tourists but lots of Greek ones, has a large number of very good restaurants. In fact I did not find a bad one. These are the restaurants we did manage to eat at in the short time we were on the island. Chios also being a relatively self-sufficient agricultural island has a good amount of fresh fruits and vegetables not to mention fresh fish and beef, pork, lamb, goat and local sausages. Those who have been to Lesvos will find the menus similar though not exactly. But if you are used to the high standard of cooking and eating on Lesvos, you should not be too disappointed with the cuisine on Chios. If you like *keftedes* (meat-balls), *tomato-keftedes*, *tiropitakis* (cheese pies), *souzoukakia* (spicy tomato covered meatballs from Smyrna in Asia Minor), *saganaki* (fried cheese), fresh fish, shrimp, squid and especially if you like them fried then you will be pretty happy on Chios. If you are looking for the *ouzo-mezedes* culture you will also find it in Chios (Check out the cafeneon in

Pirgi-photo). In 5 days it is tough to eat in enough restaurants to write an informative restaurant guide. But believe me I tried.

In Chios Town right where the ferry comes in there are several restaurants that call themselves taverna-ouzeries though I would call them *psarotavernas* (fish taverns). Our favorite one is called Tsivaeri Ouzeri and their menu featured fried gavros (anchovies), grilled sardines, fried shrimp and a number of other fish sold by the kilo or per plate. One specialty of the island is a fried dish of *atherina* which are the smallest fish, mixed with onions and flour and deep-fried into a sort of fishy-onion pancake.

Its great. They also make it with shrimp. *Liasta* is the same as *gouna* which if you have ever been to Paros you will know that it is sun-dried mackerel, seasoned and grilled. Liasta is one of those perfect foods that you eat once and crave forever. Another specialty of the island is tomato-keftedes which are deep-fried tomato balls. Oh yeah. I mentioned three restaurants in a row but there is a 4th. Its a patsa-pizza place. This is a rare combination. Patsa is a working class food made from the intestines of a sheep and is a sort of cure-all, and pizza is... well you know what pizza is. Its a unique combination. I don't think I have ever seen another *patzadidiko-pizzaria* in Greece. It may be worth checking out. I didn't but only because my wife believes that any restaurant that serves both pizza and patsa can't be any good. I disagree but as long as we are married I probably will never get to eat there.

Our first meal was at an ouzerie-mezodopoleion in Chios town called Palio Petrino which was right on the waterfront. Despite the traffic whizzing by and the smell of the harbor, Palio Petrino served some great food, many traditional Chios dishes and the rest of the stuff you will find at any modern traditional ouzerie. Fried fish, *saganaki*, grilled local cheese with peppers and tomatoes and several varieties of ouzo. *Apalarina* is the big brand and is to Chios as EPOM is to Lesvos. I liked *Kakitsis* which was recommended by Glykeria, our host. The ouzos on Chios were all good but the next few places I went to and ordered Kakitsis the waiters seemed surprised and said "Ahhhh. You know Kakatsis" like it was some island secret that tourists were not supposed to know about. From then on I ordered it, until I discovered souma. Mastika is another spirit which is made from the tree the island os known for, but it is more for after dinner.

The best place (least pretentious) for ouzo and *mezedes* is right across from the main square near the main gate of the castle where there are

several traditional cafeneons usually full of old men playing cards. Check out the Ouzerie Akropol or the Agora which both served nice mezedes. Also check in the neighborhood within the castle for the Oinomagereion Ouzeri of Jacovo E Panta or simply Iakovos. Nice local mezedes, ouzo and souma. Sometimes they have live music (unplugged), most of the times spontaneously by regular clients. Don't forget to go to Manara's Loukoumades (fried dough with honey) in the market. Also in the market is the Ellenikicousina (Greek cuisine)
Estiatorio(restaurant) which like the traditional restaurants in Athens and Mytilini, serves patsa. These market restaurants are good choices to eat at because they are for the people who work in the market so they can't get away with serving second rate meat or old fish to the guys who are selling it. Like the other market restaurants it is

open 24 hours. Check out Vyzantio in the main square.

Hotzas is considered one of the best restaurants on the island and some will go far as to say one of the best in the North Aegean. It is a family owned taverna with a nice garden though it is a good 20 minute walk from the port. Still it is worth going since you can work up an appetite going there and you can walk off the calories on the way back. It is at Georgiou Kondyli 3. Another great family owned restaurant away from the port is To Kechrimpari Mezedopoulion at Ag. Anargiron 7 a few blocks above the marketplace. In an old stone beiliding decorated with antiques and old photos they serve a number of Chios-style and Greek mezedes including fried *gavros* (anchovies), skate, mussels, *politiki salata* (like a spicy coleslaw), keftedes, fried shrimp and a variety of ouzos to wash it down with. If you have been in Greece for awhile and are tired of Greek cooking or want to take a break for the night you can try La Bussola, an Italian pizzaria-restaurant on the far side of the waterfront near the Chandris Hotel.

Tassos Taverna in the neighborhood behind the Hotel Chandris has received good reviews from Rough Guide but we never made it there to eat. I did walk by and check it out. Its in a house with a large garden and looked a lot more pleasant than the waterfront. The menu was a large one with a lot of variation and included *saligaria* (snails), *lakerda* (raw tuna), shrimp with fried onion, shrimp *saganaki*, your classic grilled and fried fish and many grilled meats, oven dishes and even pastas. It looked pretty good to me and if I had not been in such a rush to get out of Chios-town I would have eaten there. Anyway Rough Guide liked it and they seem to know a good restaurant when they see one, or hopefully eat in one. Then a week or so after I finished this Chios site I got an e-mail from someone who loved Tassos Taverna....

"Though my wife and I have been to the most Greek islands, Chios was one of those we never had a chance to visit till last week. We just returned from Chios the other day. Almost visited all the tavernas mentioned, including Tassos Taverna, which I can tell you is the only taverna worth the excellent food and the money in Chios town... and well deserved the Rough Guide review. Am really sorry that you missed the excellent food that Mr. Tassos personally sits and prepares himself. I ate twice there and met some excellent local people and on the first day was given proper info on where to eat in other villages that we planned to visit."

There are a number of fish tavernas on the waterfront of Lagada. If you have an able designated driver and have a comfortable car you can be there in half an hour from Chios-town.

In Mesta's central square the Mesaionas Taverna has a wide variety of local Chios and popular Greek foods. They have a number of oven baked dishes on display and all the usual grilled meat that you will find in any psistaria. Service is good and the restaurant usually fills up by 10pm with locals, tourists and returning Greek-Americans. Despina is a very cool taverna owner and the staff, made up mostly of cousins, brothers, sisters and friends are friendly and fun. The square is the only place to be so most people make a night of it right there, switching from the local Mestousiko wine to the excellent souma that is produced in the village. Bougiourdi is the dish in the photo which I would describe as an oven-baked Greek salad. I know that sounds disgusting but imagine putting all the ingredients of a Greek salad (except the cucumbers) and cooking it like a stew. (Sort of like saganaki I guess). Great for dipping your bread in and by the way Despina had some of the best wholegrain bread I have eaten in Greece. She uses pure and local ingredients in their cooking.

There are also a couple psistaria-pizzaria multi-purpose restaurants outside the walls of the town including Parakathi which is a pizza and pasta restaurant. The pizza is good, baked in a wood oven. Tasos, the owner, also makes nice warm sandwiches for take away, which is convenient if you want to take something to the beach.. In Pirgi the cafeneon-ouzeri with the columns in the main square is worth a visit for the traditional mezedes he serves with his ouzo.

If there was a traditional cafeneon like this in Mesta I would still be there. There is one in Olympos too.

In Emporio there are several fish taverna-ouzeri places right on the sea. The Poseidonas is owned by Michael Colombus, another descendant of the guy who discovered America and worth going to get his opinion on the controversy. Next door is the Emporios restaurant. Both serve grilled and fried fish, salads, and the usual island fare and both are good. One of them, I forget which because I took both their cards and got them mixed up, had a great big lobster tank full of some of the largest lobsters I had ever seen. I am not encouraging you to order lobsters. They are expensive and they mate for life.

The Makellos Traditional Taverna in the faraway village of Pityos is about as authentic as you will find anywhere with the ladies making their pasta and *dolmadakia* by hand. This is called *cherissia* which means 'made by hand'. People come from miles around for lunch and I suppose for dinner though driving home after a couple leaders of wine might be treacherous. Get the pasta with tomato sauce and cheese or the goat in red sauce which was fall-off-the-bone tender. Stuffed zucchini flowers are good, beautiful Greek salads, sadziki and of course the tomato-keftedes. You can also take the bus. It stops right in front of the taverna. If you have a day for exploration and you are in this part of the island, or even if you aren't, this is where I recommend you eat.

If you are on the west coast of Chios the Taverna Metoxi on the beach in Metochi Bay is a good place to stop for fresh fish, boiled marinated octopus and a very fine specimen of a Greek salad. If you can hold out until you reach Limnos, the small beach beneath Volissos there is a fish taverna on the beach there called the Limnos Taverna.

Tired of Greek food? The Golden Odyssey Hotel between Karfas and Chios-town advertises the Chinese Palace Restaurant with 82 dishes prepared by their very own professional Chinese cook, open daily and for Sunday brunch. We passed a Mexican restaurant on the way to Kardamilla. I took a photo but forgot to make a note of where the village was. Maybe somewhere near Lagada. Let me know if you find it and if it is any good.

Hotels in Chios

Chios has a large number of hotels of all different categories as well as rooms to rent. Its just a matter of deciding where you want to stay.

Chios Town

In Chios-town I stayed at the Chandris Hotel which is probably about as good as it gets, at least in town. Terrific view, nice breakfast, a pool, Greek music nights on Friday with a buffet dinner, good air-conditioning and within walking distance of just about anywhere in town. Nearby is the Grecian Castle Hotel which offers year-round accommodations in elegant rooms at pretty reasonable prices in a large mansion with a swimming pool, right on the sea. For more economical accommodations try the 2-star Diana Hotel on the waterfront which has a roof garden with views of the Aegean Sea and a snack bar. It offers air-conditioned rooms with free Wi-Fi. Porto Chios Hotel is within a short walk from the port, the castle and commercial shopping and offers tastefully furnished accommodations with free Wi-Fi and a private balcony. If you want to be close to the ferry Aegean Sea Rooms offers tasteful accommodations with free Wi-Fi access.

Campos

In Campos the Argentikon Luxury Suites have been recognized as one of the 100 Best Villas in the World I guess by Conde Naste or one of those kinds of magazines, or maybe it's a club or something. Regardless, it is hard to doubt that it is one of the 100 best villas, hotels or anything. The former mansion of the Argenti Family from Genoa, if it was not available as a hotel they could sell tickets just to visit it like the Biltmore House in North Carolina where they filmed *Being There*. It is one of the only properties I have ever seen that had a 10 rating on Booking.com. That means that everybody who stayed there absolutely loved it. So if you want to feel like royalty or Chauncy Gardner for a night or more then this is where you should stay. If they don't have availability, (which is possible so if you want to stay there book it now), it is not the only historical mansion in the area that has been converted into a fabulous hotel. Others include the Archontiko Riziko, The Voulamandis House, The Sourediko,The Topakas House and other amazing properties in Kambos which you can find on Booking.com's Kambos page

Mastic Villages

For those who want to stay in or close to the Mastic Villages I recommend a couple places. For those who don't mind spending a little extra for comfort try the Medieval Castle Suites, a hotel and apartment complex in Mesta that combines all modern facilities with the experience of living in a 14th Century village or castle. If you want something more simple but no less pleasant then Anna Floradi Apartments has studios for two or four people, with kitchenette, air-conditioning, refrigerator, running hot water, private bathroom, satelite TV and central heating fore the winter months. We stayed here and they were fine. To Petrino is a traditional 19th-century building. It features free Wi-Fi and air conditioned rooms with access to the grounds or with views of the medieval village of Vessa. Also in Vessa the Traditional Hotel Ianthe is comprised of 2 historic buildings. The Neocalssiko building was built in 1880 and the Kamarospito was built around 1750.

Emporio

In Emporio which is close enough to the Mastic Villages to visit, we stayed at the Emporio Bay Hotel which was clean, friendly, a 2 minute walk from the beaches, tavernas and the shops, had a really great swimming pool and a lot of nice people who came back year after year, always a good sign. This is probably your best bet if you want to stay on or near the sea. The family-run Haus Fay is located at the central square Emporios village, 650 feet away from the famous beaches of Mavra Volia and Foki. It offers accommodation with a private balcony and free Wi-Fi. The Mastiha Emporios Apartments offers rooms, villas and apartments right on the sea with Free wifi. Hotel Almiriki is located on Lithi Bay southwest of Chios-town. It features a sun terrace with hot tub, a beachfront café-bar, and rooms with free Wi-Fi and like Emporio Bay is close enough to visit the Mastic Villages.

Karfas

Karfas is a beach town where most of the island's hotels are located. If big hotels are your thing then Golden Sand Hotel is a Catagory A located on the sandy beach of Karfas, 7 km from the center of the town of Chios and 4 km from the airport. Built on 3 acres of waterfront property it has an Olympic sized swimming pool and 108 airconditioned rooms. Aegean Dream Hotel on the beach offers self-catered residences. It features a spa with gym and a swimming pool with free lounge chairs, towels and umbrellas. There are smaller, family run hotels as well like Evagelia Apartments which offers self-catering accommodation with a private balcony overlooking the Aegean Sea. Plaka Studios is a seafront hotel located just 500 ft from Karfas Beach. It offers rooms with kitchen and free Wi-Fi access, some enjoying panoramic views of the Aegean Sea and the sunrise. For more hotels in Karfas see Booking.com's Karfas page.

Around Chios

On a low hill right above the unspoiled sandy beach of Vokaria, Amarandos Seaview Apartments features spacious apartments with large sea-view balconies 300 feet from the small fishing harbor of the village, the seafood tavernas and cafes. Featuring a blossomed garden with bougainvillea and palm trees, the family-run Theoxenia Chios is located right on the shingle Agia Fotini Beach in Chios. Its air-conditioned units come with free Wi-Fi and offer unobstructed views over the Aegean Sea. Located in Daskalopetra, Pearl Bay Hotel Apartments offers fully equipped accommodation with a PC, free Wi-Fi, 42" LCD TV and DVD player. All Pearl Bay air-conditioned apartments and suites have a balcony, some with sea or mountain views. Each features a fully fitted kitchen with dining/living area and a spa bath. Located in Volissos, Yasemi of Chios is a traditionally built property offering self-catering accommodation with private balconies overlooking the scenic surroundings. The beaches of Lefkathia, Gonia and Limnos are less than a mile away. Closer to the sea Zorbas Apartments offers romantically decorated accommodation with kitchenette and sea views in the area of Volissos. Situated on a pine-covered hill overlooking the beautiful beach, Volissos Holiday Homes (photo) offers self-catering accommodation with sea-view verandas. It provides free Wi-Fi in some units, and it is within easy walking distance of Lefkadia beach. The port of Limnia with its cafe-bars and tavernas is a 2-minute walk. Volissos rooms are spacious and elegantly furnished. They include a fully equipped kitchen with dining area and come with a TV, air conditioning and hairdryer. Most rooms also feature a fireplace.

Top Things to see on Chios

1) Mesta: The medieval mastic village is on my top-10 for all of Greece so make sure you visit this at least.

2) Cave of Olympi: Its not Diros where you cruise around in a little boat through underground rivers, but on a hot day there is no cooler place to be and caves are always impressive anyway.

3) Pirgi: The scrafitti or *ksista* designed houses of this mastic village may have you repainting your own house after your holiday. Plus the cafeneon in the main square is one of the best.

4) Emborio: The black sand beaches are in my top ten beaches of Greece and the town is charming and peaceful except on weekends in July and August when it seems like half of Chios is here.

5) Anavatos: The deserted city where the inhabitants threw themselves from the cliffs rather than be taken by the Turks

6) Archaeological Museum of Chios: One of the best in the Greek islands and an easy walk from the waterfront in Chios town though you will probably get lost anyway

7) Nea Moni Monastery: Awe inspiring setting and beautiful wall paintings and mosaics and a feeling of peace that will give you an idea of what Mount Athos is like.

8) West coast beaches from Vroulidia to Agia Markela, take your pick. They are all beautiful.

9) The Kastro of Chios Town and while you are at it the main platia

10) Kampos: Find someone to take you around on foot and see all the beautiful mansions and greenery.

Gone through my Top-10?

Try these too from longtime Chios visitor Doortje van Lieshout from Berghem, Holland...

-Agio Gala with the Byzanthine church of Panagia i Agiogalousena built below the village in the entrance of the caves.

-The villages Kardamyla/Marmaro with a nice port and the windmill Mylo Tou Mavri.

-Ano Kardamyla, Spilia and Mountain of Gria

-Viki, Amades and Kambia with the Kambia-Canyon with view on the Pelineonmountain and surroundings

-Monastery Agioi Pateras near Nea Moni

-Monastery Agios Minas near Neohori famous in world history for the holocaust in 1822. 3500 women and children were massacred by the Turks.

-Monastery Agios Constantinos near Thymiana and Karfas, only open for women

-The village Vessa a well preserved village in the center of a big agricultiral area, the village Agios Georgios Sikousis a large village built on the top of a hill with old gates and picturesque corners with a mejestic view over Kambos, the Aegean Sea and the Asian Minor Coast and the village Zifias with the artificial lake with dam and surroundings

-The village Kalamoti with the church of Panagia Agrelopoussena

-The fisherman's place Lagada and the abondoned village Kydianta as well as Pantoukios and Sykiada with the church of Agios Isidoros in the surroundings

-The smallest village Kipouries

-The late byzantine monastery of Moundon near Diefcha with 475 beautiful paintings, all in a good condition.

Beaches in Chios

If you like beaches you will be very pleased with Chios. Whether you like long sandy beaches, with or without people, deserted coves, sand, pebbles, whatever, Chios has a beach for you. For those who have been to Greece before and are used to the Cyclades where you have a choice of a half-dozen beaches, Chios will be a feast with dozens and dozens of beaches, each different from the next. You will need a car to get to them all and you will need a month on the island if you want to swim at every one. For those who don't want to drive you can stay in Karfas, Emporio, Komi, Volissos or any of the other beach towns that have hotels. For those who choose to rent a car start anywhere and visit a beach or two a day til its time to go home. These are just a few of the many beaches in Chios. Click on them to see full-size. If you like this page please share it with your friends on Google+ and Facebook

Emporios Mavros Gialos beach

Information about Emporios Mavros Gialos beach

Mavros Gialos Beach (Mavra Volia) Chios: On the southwestern coast of Chios lies the beach of Mavros Gialos (or Mavra Volia, as it is called), in a distance of 28km west of Chios Town. Its name means *black beach* due to the black pebbles and sand that were debouched there from the volcano that is now extinct.

Thanks to this unique feature, Mavros Gialos has gained good reputation. It has an incomparable natural beauty with blue crystalline waters that are quite chilly, even in the middle of the summer. It is surrounded by rocky hills with low vegetation and greenery. The area distinguishes for the natural landscape and the relaxing surrounding.

There are no tourist facilities like umbrellas and sundecks, but it remains a cosmopolitan beach visited by many tourists every year and a great sight in Chios. The beach stretches for many meters, so it rarely gets crowded.

Karfas beach

Information about Karfas beach
Karfas Beach Chios: The beach of Karfas lies 5 km south of Chios Town, in front of the seaside settlement. It is the largest tourist resort of the island and every summer it receives many visitors. The beach has fine sand and clean waters and offers all the needed tourist facilities such as sun beds, umbrellas and water sports equipments for rent. Large hotel units, inns and

rented rooms are surrounding the beach as well as bars, cafes, night clubs and restaurants.

Vrondados beach

Information about Vrondados beach
Vrondados Beach Chios: This rather small and partly organized beach is situated 4 km north of Chios Town. It is surrounded by green vegetation and tall pine trees matching idyllically with the green crystal waters of the Aegean. Most of the tourist facilities are available here like umbrellas, sundecks and canteen for the cold drinks and snacks. It is a well-sheltered bay with thick sand and pebbles. The road leading from Chios to Vrontados is a special ride where most of the tourists follow to enjoy the natural beauty of the area. Due to the short distance, the beach is easily reachable.

Agia Fotini beach

Information about Agia Fotini beach
Agia Fotini Beach Chios: Agia Fotini is a lovely coastal settlement 15 km south of Chios Town. It is one of the most beautiful beaches of the Chios lying in a bay with a pebbled shore and crystal clear waters. The natural surrounding of vast greenery provides moments of relaxation and leisure.

The beach is partly organized with umbrellas and sundecks. The homonymous coastal settlement that stretches around the beach has a high tourist development, therefore you will find taverns and all types of accommodation. It is an ideal place to spend some days in a peaceful area with many sightseeing and easy access to the city center.

Trahili beach

Information about Trahili beach

Trahili Beach Chios: Trahili is an exotic bay with crystal waters located 20km west of Chios Town and 5km north from the village of Lithi. It is an isolated pure cove far away from the crowded beaches offering a natural beauty to the surrounding area. It is known for its clear waters and white soft sand. It is surrounded by a rocky hill covered with tall pine trees all the way down to the beach. Trahili is close to Avgonyma village and easy accessible from there. The nearest tourist facilities are found in Avgonyma.

Didima beach

Information about Didima beach
Didima Beach Chios: Didima beach, meaning *the twins* in Greek, consists of two small coves located close to the charming village of Mesta. It is located 32km southwest of Chios Town, a beach far away from the busy coasts of the

island's center. The coves with the white pebbles and crystal waters look very much alike.

The beach is completely unspoilt and secluded with steep cliffs surrounded by a natural landscape. The water quality and the secluded atmosphere captivate visitors. There are no tourist facilities near this beach and it is difficult to access with public transport.

Lithi beach

Information about Lithi beach
Lithi Beach Chios: The wonderful beach of Lithi is located in a cove, west of Chios Town, on the western coast of the island. It has soft sand and mirror-like waters. The tiny seaside settlement behind the beach is famous for its excellent fresh fish and seafood, brought by the fishermen on a daily basis. The sunrise at Lithi is astonishing and truly memorable.

Megas Limnionas beach

Information about Megas Limnionas beach
Megas Limnionas Beach Chios: Just 15km south of Chios Town, you will find the enchanting beach of Megas Limnionas. This small shore consists of shiny pebbles and thick sand. Families tend to visit the beach frequently because of its shallow and crystal clear waters.

This beach is situated among the famous spots of Chios, Agia Ermioni and Karfas. Recently, the area has been developed to a large extent, in terms of tourist facilities. As a great tourist resort, Megas Limnionas offers a wide range of hotels, studios and rooms to let. Also, there are plenty of fish taverns with delicious seafood.

Agia Irini beach

Information about Agia Irini beach

Agia Irini Beach Chios: Agia Irini is a sheltered bay located on the southwestern coast of Chios, 30 km south west of Chios Town. It is named after the church of Agia Irini, built in close distance to the beach. This is a secluded bay distinguished for its small white pebbles and the crystal waters. There are no facilities of any kind yet the beach is frequented for its pure natural landscape and the peacefulness environment. Many people also go for fishing there. Agia Irini is found between the medieval villages of Elata and Mesta, offering the visitors a great opportunity for sightseeing.

Apothyka beach

Information about Apothyka beach
Apothyka Beach Chios: Apothyka is a small and secluded beach located 38km southwest of Chios Town, close to the medieval village of Mesta (4,5km). It is a clean bay with crystal waters,

well-protected from the strong winds of the Aegean. It is surrounded by rocky hills with lush bushes and vast greenery. It is a completely unspoilt beach gifted with a unique natural beauty.

A place like this is ideal for isolation and diving in the crystalline waters. It is very popular among the people who live in the villages nearby and for tourists fond of the quiet beaches. Next to Apothyka, there is a small remote beach but the only way to reach it is on foot. The road stops 100 meters from the beach.

Lampsa beach

Information about Lampsa beach
Lampsa Beach Chios: Lampsa is a secluded beach with clean water and nice environment located 40km west of Chios Town. It is surrounded by a natural rocky landscape with low plantation. The

water is shallow and clear, ideal for children. Despite its long distance from Chios Town, the beach receives many tourists and locals who live in Volissos, the historic village where you will find plenty of accommodation and taverns to enjoy local delicacies and homemade food. There are no umbrellas and sundecks, the area offers only the beauty of the unspoilt scenery.

Lefkathia beach

Lefkathia Beach Chios: Lefkathia is a secluded beach that lies 42 km southwest of Chios town. This is truly one of the most beautiful beaches in Chios, quite organized beach with thick sand and small pebbles that reach the shore. It is well-known for its crystal clean waters and the unspoilt surrounding.

The beach is a great inspiration for various water sports and games under the sun. It has perfect conditions for the children due to the shallow waters. It is surrounded by tall pine trees that provide shade in the hot summer days and it is protected from the strong winds. Most visitors come from the close village of Volissos, a picturesque settlement that is worth a visit.

Transportation to/from Chios

There is at least one ferry a day from Pireaus to Chios. Most days the ferry boats leave Pireaus at around 6pm and arrive in Chios at the ungodly hour of 4am, too early to check into your hotel and too late to waste money paying for a full night. But if you arrive then there are cafes and restaurants that are open where you can hang out. However, I would suggest booking your hotel through a Greek travel agency and asking them to book a transfer so someone from the hotel is there at the dock waiting for you and takes you back to the hotel and if your room is not ready because somebody is in it at least you can hang out in the lobby until the breakfast room opens. And if you are staying somewhere that is not in Chios town all the more reason to book the transfer. I highly recommend using the form and a Greek travel agency especially if you are doing Chios and other islands. Making ferry connections to any island except Lesvos can be tricky.

Unless you are leaving in the afternoon get a cabin. In fact pay a little extra and get a LUX cabin. The boats to Chios and Lesvos are modern and pretty nice, though there are a couple that are not. Go for Blue Star and Hellenic Seaways if those are your choices.

There have been boats in the past between Chios and Samos, Psara, Samothaki, Kavala,

Alexandroupolis, Limnos, Ikaria, Thessaloniki, Kalymnos, Kos and Rhodes which go from once a week to several times a week. There was a boat once or twice a week from Lavrion, near Athens to the port of Mesta in Chios. Whether these boats will be running depends on the financial condition of the ferry companies that run these routes and the demand for them.

There are daily boats to Turkey and the small island of Innousses as well.

Chios has an airport with several daily flights to and from Athens on Aegean Airways.

Chios has a bus service that can get you pretty much anywhere you want to go and if you need to get closer there are taxis.

Things to See
Medieval Castle

The Medieval Castle of Chios, Greece: Initially, The Castle or Fortress of Chios enclosed the entire town of Chios. Later, the town expanded beyond the Castle walls. It was during the Byzantine period at the end of the 10th century that the first architectural phase of the monument was built. The original building has been renovated and almost nothing has survived from the initial construction. The Venetians reconstructed the Central Gate (Porta Maggiore) in 1694. You enter the Castle through this gate, located at the south end.

Ioustiniani Palace, a two-storey building stands in the enclosed area, near the gate. Kria Vrisi (Cold Fountain), the semi-subterranean water cistern built under the Genoese, and the massive tower known as *Kulas* are worth seeing.

In olden times, a wide moat surrounded the Castle. The Genoese, Venetians, and Turks, from the early 14th century until the Greek War of Independence, made a series of additions, renovations, and repairs. The main entrance of the Castle was consolidated, the facade of the building called *Dark Dungeon* was cleared, the roof was strengthened, the masonry was repaired, while the pavement is revealed after the passageway on the walls over the main gate was cleared. In present times, residents inhabit the Castle.

Maritime Museum

The Maritime Museum of Chios, Eastern Aegean: An island with rich nautical tradition, the Maritime Museum of Chios depicts the long way of the locals as seafarers. The museum is located in Chios Town and it is housed in a two-storey

Neoclassical mansion that was donated in 1991 by the shipowner Anastasios Pateras in order to host the museum. This mansion was constructed in the early 1920s and it has undergone some reformations in order to host the museum.

This maritime museum hosts portraits of sailboats and steamboats that belonged to shipowners from Chios works of the local artist Aristides Glykas (1870-1940), navigation tools, miniatures of vessels from various periods, photographs from life on board, manuscripts and many other exhibits that come from private collections. At the garden of the museum, there is a monument dedicated to the local seamen who lost their lives during World War II (1939-1945).

The Monastery of Nea Moni in Chios, Greece: The Monastery of Nea Moni is one of the oldest monasteries in Greece, located in the center of Chios island. Dating from the 11th century, the monastery was built by the Byzantine Emperor Constantine IX Monomachos and his wife Empress Zoe on the site where three monks found a holy icon.

The construction of the monastery began in 1042 and it was completed by the year 1055. Till the 17th century, the monastery had about 800 monks and much economic power with an enormous fortune, mostly land property. However, after the destruction of Chios by the Ottomans in 1822, the monastery gradually lost its prestige and the population of the monks decreased.

Now the monastery extends in an area of about 17,000 sq.m. and has only three monks. The monastery complex consists of the catholicon (main church), the cells, the dining room and a small chapel to Saint Luke, while it is surrounded by walls. Nea Moni is particularly famous for its frescoes on the walls of the churches that date from many centuries ago.

In 1990, the Monastery of Nea Moni on Chios, along with the Monastery of Hosios Loukas in central Greece and of Daphni in Athens, was included in the Unesco World Heritage monuments

Chios Olympi Cave

The Olympi Cave of Chios, Greece: The Cave of Olympi is an impressive natural attraction in Sykia area, about 35 km from Chios town and 5 km from Olympi village. This Cave is famous for its extraordinary stalactite formations. The stalactites are generally formed when water, with mixed lime content, runs off the roof and solidifies over a period of time, forming some figures. According to archaeologists, the stalactites at Olympi Cave started forming about 150 million years ago.

However, the excavations there began in 1985, by the Hellenic Speleological Company and by 2002 the cave site was already open to the public. The temperature inside the cave is stable at 18oC and the humidity is 95%. The Olympi Cave is one of the most beautiful natural monuments of Greece. The amazing stalactite decoration inside the cave exemplifies the creativity of Nature. The pattern of the fine stalactite formation gives you the feeling of a classic painting done on nature's wall.

The most curious fact about this cave is that some of the stalactites are formed in a slanting shape, challenging the law of gravity. According to scientists, this peculiar formation may be the result of the continuous downward flow of air through the openings on the roof of the rock. The calcium carbonate and the argillic contents together paint the cave in multiple colors. The gray/white calcium carbonate stone is beautified with the reddish yellow argillic earth at some places. Together they give a mesmerizing appearance to the cave.

Oinousses Island

The island of Oinousses close to Chios, Greece: Oinousses is a group of 9 small islands to the east of Chios, between the island and the Turkish shores. The main island and at the same time the harbor of the complex is Oinoussa, where the main settlement is found. The population on Oinousses does not surpass 1,000 permanent inhabitants, most of whom are occupied with stockbreeding, fishing, and seafaring.

In fact, Oinousses have always been a place with a long and rich maritime culture and many Greek ship owners come from this tiny place. These shipowner families, such as Lemos and Pateras, have contributed a lot to the island, with donations to the municipality and constructions of important works, such as a cultural center and a stadium.

The architecture of the island is traditional: red-tiled houses, paved paths and a picturesque square, with a sculpture dedicated to the Unknown Sailorman. The harbor of Oinousses is small but hosts a large number of yachts, especially in summer, and fishing boats. At the entrance of the harbor, there is a bronze mermaid to welcome the visitors and the statue of the Oinoussian Mother.

The most famous sight of the island is the Monastery of Evangelismos of the Virgin Mary. It was founded in 1964 and has some amazing frescoes, illustrated by the famous artist Fotis Kontoglou. There is also a Naval Museum, founded in 1991, which includes many interesting ship models, old naval equipment, photographs and old pieces of weapon. The island of Oinousses is daily linked to Chios town. It makes a great excursion to spend a couple of days in peace and picturesqueness.

Psara Island

The island of Psara, close to Chios, Eastern Aegean: Psara is a cluster of seven small islands in the Aegean Sea, that lies 12 miles to the northwest of Chios. The largest of them is called

Psara and it is the only inhabited island. The others are Antispara, Ai-Nikolaki, Prasonisi, Daskalio, Kato Nisi and Nisiopoula. Psara has a rocky terrain filled with hills and mountains, the highest of them being Prophitis Ilias.

Along with its history, Psara has been the site for many important historical events. It has been inhabited since the ancient times but it became known in the recent Greek history since it contributed a lot in the Greek War of Independence in the 19th century and in fact, was the third strongest Greek naval force, after Hydra and Spetses. Psara gave birth to a number of notable revolutionists including Admiral Konstantinos Kanaris and Papanikolis.

In June 1824, Psara faced a great tragedy. The Turks landed on the island and destroyed it, as a revenge for the participating to the Greek

Revolution. Out of the 30,000 inhabitants, only 3,000 were saved in small boats of the French fleet. The Turks set the whole island on fire and made Psara one of the greatest tragedies of the recent Greek history. The island never managed to recover this destruction and today it is just a small, almost isolated island of the Aegean Sea with less than 500 permanent residents.

The rocky terrain of the island does not allow them to deal with cultivation, so they depend on fishing to make their living. What Psara has to offer to visitors is a lot of tranquility. It is a lovely destination for those who wish to practice hiking and mountain biking. In fact, the peak of Profitis Ilias gives amazing views of the island. Psara does not have much tourist amenities, except for some snack bars, cafes, and rooms to let.

The most important tourist attractions are the house of Konstantinos Kanaris and some nice churches, such as the church of Agia Markella and the Monastery of the Assumption of the Virgin. Psara can be accessed by boat from Chios town and from Limnia, the port of Volissos.

Monastery of Agia Markella

The Monastery of Agia Markella in Volissos, Chios: The Monastery of Agia Markella, the patron saint of Chios, is located 8 km from the village of Volissos and 45 km from Chios Town, on the northwestern side of the island. This monastery is actually built on the beach with clean water and view to the secluded island of Psara.

A small path from the beach leads to the saint's site of martyrdom, where a large pilgrimage takes place on July 22nd, the celebration day of

Agia Markella. This day is very important for the island of Chios and thousands of visitors travel to the island for this cause. In fact, a lot of pilgrims actually walk all the way from Chios Town to the monastery of Agia Markella, a distance of 45 km, as a kind of solemn promise to the saint.

Agia Markella lived in Volissos Chios in the 14th century. Her father was a pagan and her mother was a devoted Christian, who raised her daughter as a Christian, too. At a young age, her mother died and around her 18th birthday, her father was forcing her to become an idolater. Afraid of her father, Markella ran away from her home and found refuge in the mountains.

One day, her father found her hiding in a bush and set the bush on fire to force her to come out. Markella ran to the sea to escape but her father wounded her with an arrow. The blood of the saint dyed the rocks and it is said that the faithful can see this blood on her festive day.

As she was injured, she prayed to Christ to hide her and, in fact, a rock opened and hid all her body, except for her head. Her father found her, cut the head and threw it in the sea. A water spring flows till today from these rocks. A few years later, her head was found on the close beach of Komi.

On the celebration day of Agia Markella, on July 22nd, pilgrims walk about 20 min from the Monastery to the site of the martyrdom of Agia Markella. There, the priest prays the paraclesis (pray to the saint) and the sea water below the cliff starts to boil, as the pilgrims said. This stops when the paraclesis finishes. They say that if you taste this boiled sea water that day, it will be as drinkable as pure water.

Agios Markos Monastery

The Monastery of Agios Markos in Chios, Greece: The Monastery of Agios Markos (Saint Marc) is located on a hill above Karies village, only 6 km from Chios Town. Built on the slopes of Mount Penthodos, this monastery was established in 1886 by monk Parthenios, an ascetic who was living alone in a nearby cave and was later buried inside the monastery. The current building was constructed on the ruins of an 18th-century monastery.

The monastery of Agios Markos played an important role during the struggle for freedom till 1912, when the island of Chios was finally integrated to the Greek State. Also in the early 20th century, a school of hagiography was working there. The high location of the monastery and the cave of monk Parthenios give the most beautiful view of Chios Town and the surrounding area.

Villages

Chios Pyrgi

Information about Pyrgi
Pyrgi village Chios: Pyrgi is one of the most beautiful villages of Chios located 24 km west of the island's main town, close to Mastihochoria, The area that produces the famous mastic. Today, more than 1,200 inhabitants live in Pyrgi most of whom are engaged in the production of mastic and agriculture. The village was named after the central medieval tower that still stands in the village and has maintained its traditional architecture.

Pyrgi is a really impressive and picturesque place. The facades of its buildings are decorated with grey and white geometrical shapes, which is an influence from the years of the Frankish domination on the island. Because of its unique decoration, Pyrgi is also known as "the painted village".

Like in the other medieval villages of the island, the stone houses of Pyrgi are built close one to each other, forming a defensive wall. Narrow stone-paved streets, superb churches, unique architecture and balconies full of flowers and sun-dried tomatoes are composing the magical scenery of the village. Accommodations, cafes and excellent taverns are available in the village.

Chios Mesta

Information about Mesta
Mesta village Chios: The small village of Mesta is located 35 km south west of Chios Town, in the area called Mastihochoria (Mastic Villages). Mesta used to be a heavy producer of mastic and

its inhabitants were wealthy, as testify today the beautiful mansions. It has about 400 inhabitants and is the best preserved medieval village of Chios. The houses are built attached one to another, forming a fortified wall.

This is one of the finest examples of defensive architecture. Narrow cobbled alleys are winding around the houses, leading to the lovely central square. The wonderful traditional architecture of Mesta is protected and all interventions alternating the original architectural style are prohibited. The inhabitants of the village are also preserving their traditional customs and traditions.

Chios Anavatos

Anavatos village Chios: Anavatos is a deserted village located 19km west of Chios Town. It was built on top of a hill, at an altitude of 450 meters above the sea with steep rocks, in true harmony with the natural environment. It is believed that this medieval settlement was founded for military purposes, particularly for the surveillance of the west coast of Chios. The village was abandoned after the catastrophic earthquake of 1881 and today it is a national monument for the island.

The old village preserves its Medieval frame with the fortress, the Church of Taxiarhis, the old school and the Church of Virgin Mary. In the lower part of Anavatos, there are still just a few inhabitants who welcome the visitors.

The locals demonstrate the historical place and their quality products (honey, plants, cheese and home desserts). There is a wonderful traditional coffee shop serving delicious desserts and mezedes. The village is connected with the center of Chios with a beautiful route of 45 minutes drive. There is also a great path, ideal for descent in the forest, starting from Provatas and leading to Anavatos.

Chios Volissos

Information about Volissos
Volissos village Chios: Volissos is located 38 km north-west of Chios Town and is the capital of the Municipality of Amani. It is a beautiful village, built on the slopes of a hill, at the top of which stands a byzantine tower. The walls, the towers and other ruins of a medieval castle are overlooking the village, giving it a picturesque atmosphere.

The village has a population of about 500 inhabitants, most of whom are engaged in agriculture ans farming. Some also believe that Volissos is the birthplace of the famous lyric poet

Homer. There are many things worth visiting all over the village of Volissos. Such are the Monastery of Agia Markella, the Castle and the numerous water mills and Byzantine churches. Some public services, a community clinic, accommodation, cafes and taverns are available in the village of Volissos.

Avgonyma

Information about Avgonyma
Avgonyma village Chios: The village is located 15 km west of Chios Town. It is built on top of a hill and its first inhabitants were traced back in 11th century. The surrounding area is covered with mastic trees, and olive groves. The houses are built of stone and most of them are in ruins while others were restored by their owners.

Today, there are 85 people living in Avgonyma, most of whom are engaged in agriculture.

Though the village does not have a significant monument, the traditional houses with great architecture, the charming cobbled roads and the taverns boast a romantic atmosphere to the village while preserving its Medieval ambience. The amazing sunset, the view to the Aegean Sea and Psara, the Medieval observation post (tower) and the picturesque bay of Elinda are interesting attractions for tourists.

Agia Ermioni

Information about Agia Ermioni
Agia Ermioni village Chios: Agia Ermioni is a beautiful fishing village located 10 km south of Chios Town and 3 km south of Karfas. The village has 200 permanent inhabitants and several cottages that are used for summer vacations. Over the years, the area has been quite

developed due to its idyllic surrounding and the peaceful environment.

Moreover, the traditional style of the village is highly appreciated by the tourists who enjoy spending time there. Agia Ermioni is mostly a family resort. The village offers newly-built hotels and other types of accommodation. Around the small port, there are many cafeterias and bars. The beaches in Agia Ermioni have a beautiful view to the Aegean Sea and splendid waters to swim.

Vrondados

Information about Vrondados
Vrondados village Chios: The village of Vrondados is known for its significant maritime tradition. It is situated 4 km north of Chios Town, on the western coast of the island. It has a

population of about 5,000 inhabitants and most of them are sailors.

The windmills of the village, the churches of Agios Stephanos, Panagia Erithiani and Saint Mark, and the tomb of the Greek writer, Yannis Psycharis, are worth a visit. The Monastery of Saint Stefan lies on the top of the hill in a verdant surrounding, and is ideal for those seeking freshness and calm. Accommodations, cafes, bars and taverns are available at Vrondados, as well as some fine beaches.

Olympi

Information about Olympi
Olympi village Chios: Olympi village lies in a green valley, approximately 30 km to the south west of Chios Town. The village was established in the 13th century and stands out for its remarkable architecture. The houses are built in

such a manner that the outer walls are conjoined, so that anyone facing the village will see a fortress with no visible openings, except for one door that allows people in and out of the village. This door is located at present day Kato Porta.

The narrow cobbled streets of the village and its imposing archways give you a sense of those times. The tower that stands at the center of the village is 20 meters high and was used for defense in case of a pirates attack. Today, the tower houses a nice restaurant.

The church of Agia Paraskevi, with its wooden iconostasis and valuable icons, offers visitors a remarkable sight, as does the *Trapeza* of Olympi, a two-storied medieval building. Another marvelous sight is the Cave of Olympi, located 3 km to the south west, close to Sykia village. It dates back almost 200,000 years and the cave has magnificent stalactites and stalagmites formations.

The neighbouring villages of Pyrghi and Mesta are also captivating. Mesta is a scenic village with vaulted archways. The Church of Taxiarches in Mesta portrays scenes from the Old Testament. Pyrgi is the largest of the medieval villages of Chios. On a hill near Phana beach, lie the remains of the temple of Phaneou Apollo. It is said that the statue of Apollo, that once stood there and hasn't yet been found, was made of silver and gold. If you are a trekking enthusiast, you could wander along the old Olympi and Mesta trail.

Tourist facilities such as traditional apartments are situated within Olympi village. Some of the old traditional houses have been renovated and turned into guesthouses, to give visitors a feel of the traditional charm. The area around Olympi is also abundant in mastic trees. These trees constitute the trademark of Chios island and are an important financial source for the island. These trees have an aromatic resin that is used in varnishes, adhesives, astringents and condiments. The nearest beaches to Olympi are Didima, Mavra Volia, Trahili, Kato Phana and Agia Dynami. They are all unique and can be easily reached from the main road.

Emporios

Information about Emporios
Emporios village Chios: This picturesque port lies 28 km south west of Chios town and 6 km from Pyrgi. This small, isolated seaside village is well-known for Mavra Volia and Foki, two wonderful beaches with black sand and pebbles that have debouched from the extinct volcano of Psarona.

For the sand lovers, there is the beach of Komi, in a distance of 2 km from Emporios. There are many traditional taverns around the lovely port serving excellent local dishes. Emporios is a place of great historical importance.

Archaeologists have found there remains from prehistoric settlements. The famous area of Dotia is overgrown with mastic trees and it is a lovely site that the visitors should not miss. In this area there are also the remains of a Medieval castle, one of the few sites in Emporios.

Kampos

Information about Kampos
Kampos village Chios: This beautiful village lies only 5 km south of Chios Town. It is the closest village to the airport and one of the few places in Chios that preserves its medieval character, despite the fact that is situated close to the

capital. Kampos has recently been proclaimed by the Ministry of Culture as a historical site. The historical course of the village begins from the Byzantine times, where most of the mansions were built but they were later ruined by the catastrophic earthquake of 1881.

Today, there are many Neoclassical houses with traditional architecture which are well-preserved through time. Every mansion and estate is considered a unique masterpiece with exceptional architecture and most of them are two-stored with great gardens and colorful terraces. The surrounding area is covered with citrus trees and mastic trees. The narrow streets and the typical architecture of the stone houses are the most important features of this beautiful settlement.

Kataraktis

Information about Kataraktis

Kataraktis village Chios: On the southwestern coast of the island, approximately 12 km from Chios Town is the seaside village of Kataraktis (whose name means *waterfall* in Greek). This is a very beautiful coastal settlement, combining the greenery of the mountain with the blue of the sea. Even though the houses are few and do not follow the famous Medieval architecture of Chios, still the village reveals a special beauty.

During the last years, Kataraktis has developed in tourism. There is a small port were all the fishing boats are moored. The surrounding region is covered with olive groves and mastic trees, the trademark of the island. The village has a population of about 450 inhabitants and due to the reduced mastic production many of the young locals are occupied with shipping and construction works in Chios Town.

Kataraktis has a lovely beach and many traditional taverns serving the best seafood. It is an ideal place for quiet, family vacations. Closeby, there is the monastery of Panagia Rouxouniotissa that was built during the Medieval times. The old, abandoned village of Kataraktis is built 2km southwest of the village. Today it is deserted, yet it is an important pole of attraction for many visitors due to its medieval houses and the Byzantine churches.

Karyes

Information about Karyes
Karyes village Chios: The beautiful village of Karyes is built amphitheatrically on the slopes of a hill, 6 km north west of Chios Town. Karyes has about 650 inhabitants. It is famous for the breathtaking view it offers and for its spring waters which are the best of the island.It has a

rich vegetation, a fine climate and a great variety of aromatic herbs.

Every summer, the cultural society organizes various dances and festivities in the village square, which attract a lot of visitors. Accommodations, traditional cafes and fine taverns are available in Karyes.

Kardamyla

Information about Kardamyla
Kardamila village Chios: Kardamila is located at 28 km north-west of Chios Town and is divided into two settlements. Kato and Pano Horio (Low and Upper Village) which is the older part of the village and spreads at the feet of a steep hill, in a region full of plane trees.

Some fine examples of the traditional architecture of the island are standing here, surrounded by narrow alleys and passages with stone arcades.

The other part of Kardamila is Kato Horio (Lower Village), also called Marmaro, where one will be able to admire the superb traditional mansions built of stone and decorated with flowers and plants. Each settlement has about 2,000 inhabitants

Michael Lopez

The End